CW00405635

DAVID CLA... minister fo... mining vil... Sheffield, and for six years in inner London. In 1973 he took up the post of Senior Lecturer in the Community and Youth Work Department at Westhill College, Birmingham, in recent years specializing in the field of community education.

David Clark believes passionately that the church's task is to bear witness to the dynamic life of the kingdom. He sees the creation of community as the heart of this task, and the coming into being of a wide diversity of Christian cells as essential for its fulfilment. To help put his convictions into practice he has edited the magazine *Community* since 1971, and has been Director of the National Centre for Christian Communities and Networks since 1981. In 1977 he wrote *Basic Communities – Towards an Alternative Society*, published by SPCK, and in 1974 *The Liberation of the Church – the Role of Basic Christian Groups in a New Re-formation*, published by the National Centre.

David Clark is married, with a son and a daughter. His family and his many other interests – climbing, ornithology, sport, travel – are for him an integral part of the rich life of the kingdom about which he writes in this book.

she worked as a Methodist
minister for five years in Woodhouse, a
Leeds suburb, on the outskirts of

DAVID CLARK

Yes to Life

In Search of the Kingdom Community

Collins
FOUNT PAPERBACKS

First published in Great Britain in 1987
by Fount Paperbacks, London

Copyright © David Clark 1987

Made and printed in Great Britain by
William Collins Sons and Co. Ltd, Glasgow

To all fellow
travellers

Contents

Introduction

In 1984 I wrote a book called *The Liberation of the Church* which was published by the National Centre for Christian Communities and Networks of which I am the Director. It described the parlous state in which I felt that the institutional church in the United Kingdom now found itself. But it was also about the growth of a new Christian movement, still in the early stages of its development, offering genuine hope for the future.

This movement was made up of Christians, of all denominations and none, seeking a new quality of community life. They believed that for the whole church to be engaged in this search it had to be re-created by the endeavours of small groups and networks working from the bottom up. The aim, however, was not the salvation of the church, but the transformation of society into the kingdom of God.

The Liberation of the Church is a detailed and well documented book, written with objectivity but not without passion. I still believe that it is a book of considerable importance, not because I wrote it but because of the profound changes going on within the life of the church to which I refer. But it is a book which needs to be read carefully and thoughtfully if its message is to be clearly understood.

This book deals with the same subject in a different way. It is not an autobiography but contains a good deal about those experiences in my own life which have compelled me, in company with many others, to go in search of a new quality of community life for our generation; the kingdom community, as I call it here.

This is not a neat book with all the ends tied up. I wrote it whilst still uncertain about some of the judgements I was

9

making and at times confused about the shape of things to come. I dip into my own past to illustrate the origins of my convictions but, as with any human being, my vision is limited by my own history. There is a great deal of what matters to me in life not mentioned in what follows. None the less, I am convinced that without our renewed search for the kingdom community which I examine here, and the discoveries promised to those who seek, abundant life for our planet and for ourselves will be denied.

In this book I have written mainly about myself and about the church. Some may feel that the salvation of society is far more important, and I could not agree more, as I indicate in the final chapter. But I believe that the true church, as servant and herald of the kingdom community, remains of crucial importance in the divine plan. We are called to seek its rebirth, not for our sake or for the church's sake, but for God's sake and the kingdom's sake. The kingdom is not dependent on the church, but whilst the latter remains captive the coming of the former is continually hindered.

I offer this book as one pausing to take stock of the next stage of the journey, for himself and for fellow travellers in search of the kingdom community. If it helps to encourage the reader to press on, assured that he or she is not lost, misguided or alone, I shall be more than satisfied.

David Clark
Birmingham
July 1986

CHAPTER 1

"Yes" to Life

1. Life

When I was a boy I was fascinated by a concrete paving-stone outside our house, which for no apparent reason gradually began to tilt over whilst all the others remained stolidly level. After some weeks the cause of the upheaval revealed itself. A tiny shoot from the roots of a poplar tree growing in our garden had burrowed its way under the fence and, as it sought the light of day, made easy work of pushing aside the heavy slab.

One springtime, walking in Langstrath Dale in the Lake District, I was enthralled by the sight of two sheepdogs, ears pricked to catch the shepherd's whistle, crouching and racing, twisting and turning with breathtaking vigour, to bring the flock down from the high fells for shearing. On a hot summer's day a year or two later I sat, not many miles away, on the ridge of High Street fascinated by the acrobatics of myriads of swifts as they skimmed past on a warm updraft of air from Bleawater far below, getting themselves into shape for their arduous journey south.

During a summer family holiday in the Isle of Arran we were encamped on a quiet beach when round a corner appeared a stark naked little boy of about three racing towards us. He wobbled happily along, his long fair curls bouncing up and down, with a rapturous smile all over his face. A few moments later a breathless young mother appeared in hot pursuit, caught him up and swept him into her arms, to carry him back to his point of departure, his legs still kicking, and gurgling with excitement.

11

Tracey called today. She was trying to sign up members for a mail order book club. Her patter did not impress me very much and the catalogue showed the usual glossy, pictorial volumes which are always more for show than serious reading. But she nearly persuaded me to sign on the dotted line simply because she was so friendly, vivacious, open and full of enthusiasm about her task.

Stanley always used to amaze me. He had suffered from polio when a child, and later lived on his own in the two downstairs rooms of an old terraced house in Woodhouse Mill, on the edge of Sheffield. His left side was completely paralysed, he could only get about by crawling along the floor, and his speech was badly slurred. As a member of one of my churches I visited him regularly, always expecting to have to encourage him and cheer him up because of his sedentary, enclosed and often painful existence. Yet it was usually I who came away with my spirits raised. For Stanley was not only an avid follower of the news and engaged me in long and interesting conversations. He also had a great sense of fun, on several occasions nearly falling off his dilapidated old chair with laughter.

In July 1953 I found myself in the main hall of Nottingham High School for my last school assembly, for the last time singing with gusto the school hymn and for the last time seeing the familiar faces of my school friends around me. My school years had been a mixture of hard work and energetic sport, of failure and achievement, of despair and enjoyment, of gloom and laughter. Yet in that last moment as a schoolboy I felt both the joy and the pain of being one of a company of young people who for many years had shared a unique part of life together, and now had to go their very different ways.

Such peak experiences, and many more like them, have through the years stopped me in my tracks and compelled me to gaze and reflect, to feel and wonder. They have always been unplanned and unexpected. They have always come as a kind of revelation to lift me out of my self-centred ponderings into a wider and richer dimension of life. "Surprised by joy" was the way C.S. Lewis described such moments, in his autobiography.[1] So it has been for me. They have been glimpses of what life at its fullest is all about.

For me, these experiences have nearly always been associated with some specific time and place, person or creature – the poplar root, sheepdogs in action, swifts on the wing, a small child, a door-to-door saleswoman, a polio victim, a school assembly. They have been more tangible than abstract, more sensual than cognitive. They have usually been associated with ordinary things or people which, though in themselves not especially notable or attractive, have suddenly become the medium of the extraordinary.

When these moments have come my way, they have been what Rosemary Haughton calls "an exchange of life".[2] Not only when I chatted to Stanley or to Tracey, but when no words have been spoken, a flow of energy between those of us participating in the momentary drama seems to have occurred. Even when nobody else has been present I have felt myself to be not just an observer, but an integral part of an entire happening. It has been as though I, together with all the other actors, have been caught up into a whole new world, yet one in which each of us has a vital part to play. It is as if one "Yes" to life is met and enriched by many other "Yeses".

Such experiences are a kind of falling in love. They may at times be like a wild embrace; at others like a gentle caress. They can be demonstrative love affairs, as when four of us once legged it down Glencoe after a hard day's climbing on Bidean nam Bian, singing at the top of our voices. They can be love affairs intense yet fragile, as when, sitting on a log in a Surrey wood in the glittering sunshine of an early spring morning, I dared hardly breathe, let alone speak. But whatever the mood, each experience brings a passionate awareness of and exchange of life.

I have recently returned from an Easter holiday in Borrowdale. Our room commanded a magnificent view across Derwent Water to Skiddaw, standing tall and resplendent with snow covering its summit plateau. On our last evening I watched the setting sun cast its constantly changing rays across the lake, turning the snow on Skiddaw first pink, then orange, then crimson. It was a moment, like many others before it, which I longed to hold on to for ever. Yet nothing could prevent its passing – no photographer however skilled, nor artist however talented.

These peak experiences, these changes of life, these love affairs, are ever coming and ever going. They cannot be preserved for posterity. They are vividly real yet insubstantial, they are deeply satisfying yet always make us long for more, they are down-to-earth yet transcendent. They reveal that life is not only about being but becoming; that it is not only about the present but still has to come in all its fullness.

These experiences have given me a glimpse of what I believe Christians mean by "the hope of glory". They seem to reveal a world, as real as it is timeless, wherein those things that prevent, or all too soon check, a transforming exchange of life will be overcome; wherein the different facets of human existence, which so easily and so often fragment and fall apart, will be brought together in a life-enhancing and dynamic whole. They are what Michael Wilson calls "a foretaste of wholeness to come".[3] It is towards the search for such wholeness, for the fulfilment of myself and of all else around me, for the promise of life at its richest, that the poplar shoot, the sheepdogs, the swifts, the bubbling three-year-olds, the Traceys and the Stanleys, and the true colleagueship of this world impel me.

14

2. Signs Along the Way

I have always been intrigued by those pictures which do a "switch" whilst one is looking at them. There are steps which turn inside out, there is the goblet which suddenly changes into the profile of two faces, there is the portrait of the gnarled old woman which all at once becomes a beautiful young lady, and many more.

Though none of us can yet comprehend the nature of the wholeness towards which our peak experiences point, the pictures that "switch" may give us some clue as to how we get there. Because such experiences embrace both being alive and becoming alive, they indicate that the end of our journeying comes nearer as we discover more about, and are able to express, the whole of the picture. It is a picture of what our planet can become, of what each one of us, as an individual, child, woman or man, can become, and of what every society and nation might be like. It is also a vision of what all these, being and becoming together, might achieve. It is the hope of glory.

Peak experiences which come through the sights and sounds of the natural world are to me signs of the glory that our planet is meant to reveal. The essence of that glory is that it is life-giving, expressed by sheepdogs racing over the fells and swifts darting through the air. It is the glory of the re-creation of our world every spring, as daffodils flood the Lakeland valleys and apple blossom the orchards in the Vale of Evesham. It is also the glory of the dying of our world every autumn, as the trees in the forests of mid-Wales turn a riot of browns and yellows and golds, and the hips and haws stain the hedgerows of this part of Warwickshire bright red.

I am aware that rebirth and dying contain suffering and pain as well as beauty and joy. I know that the eagle devours the lamb, that the fox plays with the dead rabbit and that the hyena tears out the stomach of the zebra. I am aware that there is nothing romantic about the devastation caused

15

by the forest fire, the erupting volcano and the violent earthquake. I stand horrified and bewildered by such events. But they do not negate my conviction that the vision of what our planet is meant to become lies in experiences of a life-giving and not a life-denying kind. I even dare to believe that at least some of that suffering and pain is an integral and creative part of the whole life-giving process; that a "Yes" to life can be spoken in the darkness as well as in the light.

Those experiences of exchanging life which have been mediated to me through my fellow human beings – the Stanleys, the Traceys and countless others – are for me signs of the glory of each man and each woman. The essence of these signs is that they are liberating, as seen in the naked three-year-old racing free and fearless along the beach. They reveal the glory of physical liberation, which comes from years of practice, enabling us to play a Beethoven piano concerto or hit a drive long and straight off the first tee. They point to a liberation of mind, which sends the crossword buff into ecstasy because of a tough clue solved, or thrills the computer addict because of a difficult programme well designed. They reveal the glory of spiritual liberation, which comes from genuine forgiveness and true reconciliation. They demonstrate the glory of human love, which makes us feel that we are valued and belong.

This kind of liberation is the theme of a parable, written some fifteen or so years ago by Richard Bach, about a seagull called Jonathan who dares to risk flying at a "terminal velocity" (for seagulls) of "two hundred and fourteen miles per hour".[4] With immense exhilaration and sense of fulfilment Jonathan comes through unscathed, liberated from the fears and restrictive practices of his cautious colleagues. The story is dedicated "to the real Jonathan Seagull, who lives within us all". But there is a sting in the tail. For his daring, but above all for his audacity, Jonathan is expelled from the flock. To break the rules of the air is to set himself apart from his fellows. The glory of liberation often carries with it the penalties of non-conformity and the loneliness of rejection. It can bring suffering as well as acclaim.

As with the planet, so in the case of human beings, we here encounter the shadow side of our existence. We find that peak experiences are matched by valley experiences. These can come, as in Jonathan's case, because we seek to be free and whole, and encounter powerful resistance. They can also come because we refuse freedom and wholeness; our ability to exchange life and to love one another seems to be matched by our readiness to deny life and to hate.

The nature of this shadow, which we sometimes call evil, is, like goodness, a mystery. Yet it, too, may in some paradoxical way have its place in the creative order of things. I believe that the power of evil is the power of goodness perverted or suppressed; that the energy which pervades cruelty is that of mercy misused; that the strength of hatred comes from that of love gone sour; and that death derives its power from life denied. If this is so, then the purpose of our journeying is not to seek to destroy the dark side of human experience, but to find ways of transforming it so that it can nourish and enrich, rather than conflict with and negate, the glory that is within each of us.

An attempt by those engaged in the field of gestalt therapy to write their own form of the Beatitudes may give a glimpse of the complementarity of "good" and "evil", and of the wholeness that can come from a recognition of this:

> Blessed are the day-dreamers for they shall find their direction.
> Blessed are the *aware* agressors, for they shall save us from destruction.

Blessed are those who can experience disgust, for they shall discover appetite.

Blessed are those who know they hate, for they shall be able to love.

Blessed are those who can endure the impasse, for they shall experience surprise.

Blessed are those who listen, for they shall hear life.

Blessed are those who can keep silent, for they shall spare us their projections.

Blessed are those who are present in their words, for they shall communicate.

Blessed are those who love their neighbours as themselves, not more, not less.[5]

There are also peak experiences which come to us, not on the mountain top, but in the midst of the multitude, such as the deep sense of comradeship I felt at the last assembly of my school life. For me, these are signs of the glory of the unity of humankind. These signs are found within the family that stays with relationships and welcomes the many challenges of living in partnership. They are found within the group which works hard or plays hard together. They are found within the nation which possesses a strong sense of common purpose, such as our own country during the last world war. And now and then they give us a fleeting glimpse of an even wider unity, on occasions such as the Olympic Games.

As with our planet and with individuals, the glory of unity is often marred. There is that within all groups and all nations which makes them quick, if not eager, to oppress, persecute and destroy. The glory of one world is obliterated by the disaster of human divisions; man against woman, white against black, West against East, North against South.

Even so, the vision of one world remains. It drives us on despite our failures, not simply for the sake of survival, though that is a strong enough motive, but because there is that in us which cannot rest content with disunity and enmity. There is a growing awareness, too, that the very forces which would separate us, partisan loyalty and sectarian solidarity, are the forces of life and love turned in on themselves. Thus, the purpose of our journeying is not to seek the destruction of these introverted expressions of corporateness, but an exchange of life which can lessen insecurity and fear and enable the boundaries of trust and fellowship to be widened. It is an immense task; indeed, what much of our race's struggle for a more human world has been about. But if the power of unity, however presently abused, has the potential to bring about a more all-embracing sense of oneness, then our peak experiences derive from much more than romantic fantasy.

3. Community – The End of our Journeying

These experiences give us some insight into what life at its fullest might be like, "rumours of angels"[6] as Peter Berger calls them. They are glimpses of the potential glory of this planet, of each woman and man, and of every group and nation. Yet the hope of glory at its zenith embraces all these manifestations, all these rumours of its presence. This greater glory I describe as the glory of community, the essence of which is the interdependence of each and every thing.

I gained as deep an appreciation as at any time of the rich interdependence of planet, individuals and groups, and the strength of community it could engender, when, from 1962 to 1967, I was the Methodist minister in Woodhouse. Woodhouse was a large "suburban village" with a population of some 10,000 residents and lay five miles south-east of the centre of Sheffield. It had originally been a farming, then a mining village, independent and thriving until incorporated into Sheffield in 1921. From the 'fifties onwards, council house estates had sprung up all round Woodhouse and, by the late 'sixties, families from slum-clearance areas in the heart of Sheffield made up nearly half of its population.

During my time there, a substantial number of the older residents who had lived in Woodhouse all their lives still exercised considerable influence. For them Woodhouse had been all that a community should be. It had provided a place in which to live, to work and to play. Over the years the natural features of the neighbourhood and the physical fabric of the village had come to embody many rich memories. The farms and the mines, "Sally Clark's" (a field at the top of the village where residents frequently went to picnic), the "Cross Daggers" pub in the village square, and the churches and chapels which were all built in the nineteenth century, symbolized their hopes and fears, their joys and sorrows.

The life of Woodhouse was further enriched for older residents by village characters who still gave warmth and zest to life. In my time these included people such as Hilda, who spent her life as an unpaid Good Samaritan giving countless hours to help the housebound and nurse the sick; Edwin, whose family had been in the undertaker's business for generations; and "old Mrs Hardcastle", who had been choir mistress at the Wesleyan Methodist church for fifty years. These and many other personalities continued to give Woodhouse an ethos rich in the diversity of human beings.

Over the years, the old villagers had been drawn together by the great events of local life. Christmas had once seen the pubs and churches packed to overflowing, and Whitsuntide was the occasion for the annual Sunday School procession, in which nearly all the village children and many parents participated. The "feast" each August had also been a week of holidaying and revelry in which all shared.

The interaction of physical environment, personalities

and local groups and associations, created a communal whole which, despite the hardships and limitations of village life, enabled old residents to find a strong sense of security, of significance and of solidarity. To these inhabitants it was *our* landscape, *our* village and *our* community.

By the time I appeared on the scene, however, there was another side to the story. The glory of old Woodhouse, at least as the elderly had experienced it, seemed to be fading fast. Neglect and demolition of the old village, the encroachment of council estates and the appearance of hundreds of "incomers" on the streets and in the shops were changing the character of the place.

Some old residents died as a result of having to move from their homes, cramped and poor as they were, into modern flats; as the fabric of the village was destroyed by the bulldozer, so too it seemed were the lives of the natives. The contribution that an individual could make to village life was increasingly restricted or ignored. Social and health workers moved in to take over the roles of the Hildas of the old world, large commercial firms threatened Edwin's undertaker's business, and the churches were regarded as relics of the past by most newcomers.

At the same time, the great corporate festivals were declining fast. There was no longer any "feast" to enable the whole village to celebrate together, the Whitsuntide procession was made up of a handful of the faithful, and the Christmas festivities had lost much of their spontaneity and carefree fun. Though the older residents retained a strong sense of community, its glory appeared to be more that of the sunset than the sunrise.

Even so, whilst the shadows seemed to be lengthening across the face of old Woodhouse, there were for those who could discern it signs of a new dawn. The recently built estates were no beauty spots like Sally Clark's had been, but they were giving a fresh lease of life to scores of families from the slums of Attercliffe and Brightside. For many children they were becoming as much "home" as the back-to-backs and terraces were "home" to the old Woodhouse residents. Personalities and characters were appearing again – in the clubs, tenants' associations and sports organizations, as well as managing the new shops. A new sense of solidarity slowly began to develop, even though it was now focused as much on communities of interest as community of place. One experience of community had begun to ebb, but another had begun to flow.

It would be foolish to overplay the glory of community life revealed in either the old or the new Woodhouse. There were, as always, those people and happenings which worked against an exchange and enrichment of life. And the threat of an ugly, impersonal and fragmented Woodhouse hung over the neighbourhood during most of my time there. Yet my years in Woodhouse led me to two helpful insights about the nature of community.[7]

The first was its sheer tenacity. Though its outward forms seem to change, community is rarely destroyed. It may wax and wane but somehow it nearly always remains, be it manifest or latent, to sustain and enrich life. I believe this is because, important as are a life-giving planet, liberated individuals and groups working together, it is community which draws them into an organic whole. This gives community a strength far greater than the sum of its parts.

None the less, I also came to believe that without a strong sense of community human beings wilt and begin to die. Community is the foundation of human society, the zenith of interdependence, the epitome of wholeness; in fact, the end of our journeying. As Parker Palmer writes, "Community means more than the comfort of souls. It means, and has always meant, the survival of the species."[8] Without a continuing and an enriching experience of community, as well as a vision of its glory to keep us moving forward, all of us eventually perish.

22

4. Where Does the Journey Begin?

The journey towards the fulfilment of planet, individuals and groups, with each making their distinctive contribution to the communal whole, is frequently empowered by a vision. The fact that this vision has often been about a city, and not simply a rural paradise, encourages me to believe that the end of our journey is a realistic one for today, not mere nostalgia for the past.

But whose vision do we heed? There are many to hand, a good number of which seem authentic enough. We might begin with visions transmitted to us from the past but, because of the passage of time, now embodied as much within our culture and our traditions as anywhere else. The problem here is that once such visions become part and parcel of everyday life, they can lose their ability to point us towards subsequent stages of the journey.

When one of my Methodist churches in Woodhouse was built, it was equipped with what then must have been seen as a magnificent coke-fired boiler. For most of my time there this boiler was looked after by a dedicated caretaker who, faithful to the call of duty, had for several decades risen at an unearthly hour each Sabbath to ensure that the congregation did not shiver. Nobody questioned this practice, nor the personal sacrifice involved to keep the church warm. Before I left the village, the caretaker reached retirement. Within a few weeks of his finishing, the leaders of the church had decided to install an oil-fired heating system requiring a minimum of maintenance, with a pre-set timing device to get it going early on a Sunday morning.

If to rely overmuch on the visions which inspired our forefathers has its problems, why not espouse the visions of the present? After leaving Woodhouse I moved to be Methodist minister in West Greenwich for six years. It was like experiencing a timewarp. It seemed to me that south-east London was a quarter of a century ahead of

Woodhouse, with West Greenwich a thriving cosmopolitan neighbourhood, diverse yet dynamic in its composition and culture. None the less, in the late 'fifties the architect designing new housing to replace that which was old and inadequate, or had suffered from war damage, hit on the brilliant idea of building high-rise flats. In this way land could be saved to give open space for lawns and playgrounds.

A number of my church members lived in such flats. When I visited them I saw that the vision had been far from glorious. The flats had worn badly and were suffering a host of problems, from misfitting windows to lifts that regularly broke down. The stairways were covered with litter and sometimes excretion, and the walls with graffiti. The residents felt isolated and lonely, and the flats on the bottom floor were subject to frequent break-ins. Many of those living there longed for their old cramped terraced houses again, for neighbours they knew and on whom they could rely.

Tradition on the one hand and modernity on the other offer us far more by way of communal visions than outmoded coke-fired boilers and badly designed high-rise flats. But the problems of relying too much on past or contemporary fashions remain. Modernity, in particular, brings further confusion by the rapidity with which new ideas can be transmitted and through the bewildering array of visions constantly being marketed. How then do we survive what Peter Berger calls this "vertigo of relativity"?[9]

I believe, as does Berger, that the only way we can find our bearings for the journey ahead is to trust our own visions. We have to go forward on the basis of our own "Yes" to life, though shared with and nourished by the "Yes" to life of others. Berger calls this accepting "the heretical imperative"; the necessity of determining for ourselves which of our peak experiences is authentic, and on that basis deciding the direction in which we must travel.

Thus the journey towards wholeness, interdependence, community has to begin with your vision and my vision of life. But it is only a beginning. For the journey entails our continuing "Yes" to life and our continuing "Yes" to life together.

5. The Journey Itself

The journey towards community is one of continuing discovery. We know little about the route ahead. We are not on an expedition where we carry a detailed map with us and an itinerary which tells us precisely when we will arrive at scheduled stopping-off points or even at our destination.

Nearly fifty years ago a group of men from inner-city Glasgow, many of them unemployed, travelled to the Island of Iona, off the west coast of Scotland, to begin rebuilding the living quarters of the famous abbey there. They were inspired and led by George MacLeod, a minister of the Church of Scotland who had been appalled by the soul-destroying nature of the unemployment and poverty in his parish of Old Govan. His conviction was that work undertaken in a spirit of comradeship, even if wages were minimal, could be both purposeful and re-creative. As a result the Iona Community came into being to provide a vision of what the sharing of experience, skills and friendship might offer to society as a whole.

In 1966 the renovation of the abbey was completed. There was pride in the considerable achievement. But then the question arose as to what next should be a focus for the work of the Iona Community. For some years there were doubts and uncertainties until gradually a new emphasis emerged. The community discovered that their original destination was in fact only a stage on the journey.

In what I have written so far I have spoken of "the end of our journeying", of our "destination" and even our "destiny". The truth is, I believe, that our "Yes" to life and to life together is, as the Iona Community came to grasp, a never-ceasing process of discovery. We are involved not in a clear-cut programme such as renovating an abbey, which has a finite end (though such programmes may help us on the way), but in a continuing process of learning about and creating community.

In this sense we never "arrive", there is no "end" to our journeying. Indeed the journey itself becomes "end" and "destination". We do not become bored or tired with this journey because we are given continuing inspiration and strength by the sheer vitality of life exchanged. "'Life' in this context", writes Rosemary Haughton, "means all of reality, apprehensible and inapprehensible, all that is and all that could be, and it involves thinking of everything, not just a part of an infinitely complex web of interdependence, but as a *moving web*, a pattern of flowing, a never-ceasing in-flow and out-flow of being."[10] The journey to which we are called is to become part of this life-giving and love-creating process of communal growth and fulfilment for which our whole universe also exists.

To say "Yes" to life and to participate in this journey demands commitment and tenacity, as does any attempt to build true community within the family, the neighbour-hood, the city or the nation. It is a pilgrimage which re-quires what Paul Tillich calls "the courage to be". Because it is a process of self-fulfilment it necessitates "the courage to be as oneself", and because it is a process in which all things are coming to fulfilment it demands "the courage to be as a part".[11] I would add a third requirement; it needs "the courage to be one with the planet", to recognize our affinity with the natural as well as the social world to which we belong.

Because this journey is as demanding as any we under-take, I would be the first to settle at home by the fire with my slippers on if it were not for three things. One is my conviction that to refuse to say "Yes" to life is in effect to say "Yes" to death. If we do not choose life, opt for a wholesome planet, choose to become fully human as individuals, as groups and as societies, strive to build community, then we choose death, to be less than human, to create chaos. There is no fence to sit on, no route between the narrow way to salvation and the broad road to destruction. We are either a part of the life-giving and love-creating purposes of the universe or we negate them.

The second thing is that there are many fellow travellers, and they come from many different and unexpected quarters. In a particularly fraught stage of my own journey, when I had doubts that I would make even the next few steps, I was given hope and strength by a Jewish woman whom I met quite unexpectedly on a train journey. She turned out to live fairly near to me, and for a year or more she walked alongside me offering encouragement, comfort and healing. She was as great a source of help as anyone could have been.

The third thing that impels me to get out of my armchair and put on my boots is my conviction that the journey is undertaken not only with human companions but with a divine guide. Indeed, if it were not for my belief that life and love and wholeness and community were all gifts of God, offered by one who shares the journey with us, I would have given up the expedition long ago.

My mother, knowing my love of mountaineering, once passed on to me a prayer (whose author I do not know) which I have kept because, in a simple yet profound way, it sums up why I stay with the journey:

Make me to be Thy happy mountaineer,
  O God most high,
My climbing soul would welcome the austere:
  Lord crucify
On rock or scree, or cliff or field or snow
The softness that would sink to things below.

27

Thou art my Guide, where Thy sure feet have trod
   Shall mine be set.
Thy lightest word my law of life O God:
   Lest I forget
And slip and fall, teach me to do Thy will,
Thy mountaineer upon Thy holy hill.

It is the presence of a divine fellow traveller that makes my
"Yes" to life, and the often hazardous journey which
follows, possible.

CHAPTER 2

"Yes" to God

1. The Creator

Galdhöpiggen is the highest mountain in Norway. It stands in the midst of the imposing Jotunheimen range. At three o'clock on a July morning in 1956, I was on its summit with two companions, watching the sun rise.

The previous day had been wet and miserable. We had climbed the peak in mist and rain, but gained little from our efforts except the satisfaction of having reached the top. Cold and disappointed, because it was our last day on the hills before returning to Oslo, we descended to a mountain hut several thousand feet below.

At about ten that night the mist had suddenly cleared and the clouds lifted. As a half-hearted joke one of my friends suggested it might be worth going up again to see the dawn. Many a true word spoken in jest! Watched by Norwegians who thought we were crazy, we pulled on our sodden boots and damp climbing jackets and, grasping ice axes and a saturated rope, set off somewhat apprehensively into the night. We traversed a large glacier in the light of the full moon and then began the arduous ascent of the ice-covered rocks leading up to the summit. We reached the top tired but triumphant and took shelter in a tumble-down cabin.

An hour or so later the first light of dawn appeared. Despite twenty degrees of frost we watched spellbound as the sun climbed stealthily over the grey cotton wool clouds which lay along the vast horizon, transforming the sky into reds and golds, blues and turquoises. Snow-capped peak after peak was stained pink, orange, purple as the ball of fire thrust its rays further and further across the mass of rugged peaks surrounding us.

My companions would not have called themselves religious people. But in the silent beauty of that Norwegian dawn we all seemed to share a sense of awe as the Creator of the universe once again performed the daily miracle of bringing light out of darkness. For me words spoken unfeelingly scores of times suddenly came breathtakingly alive: "Holy, holy, holy, Lord God of hosts; heaven and earth are full of thy glory . . ."

Back home in Birmingham there is a short walk, some fifteen minutes' drive from where we live, which I manage to cover once or twice a week. It is along a track which winds its way past farms and a pond, through woods, along the side of two small reservoirs and across open fields. Though I have now covered the ground hundreds of times it is never the same twice.

I enjoy it best in the spring. Wobbly lambs suddenly appear in the fields. One meadow is packed with a multitude of daffodils. Cowslips cover the banks of one of the reservoirs. And I know where first the chiffchaff, then the willow warbler and later the blackcap will appear, having made their arduous journey from Africa.

If dawn over the Jotunheimen gave me a glimpse of the God who brings light out of darkness, my local walk in the spring reminds me of the same God who brings life out of non-life. If sunrise over the mountains of Norway spoke of the God who created a majestic universe, my nearby stroll speaks of a Creator who brings to birth the small and the fragile, in their own way just as beautiful and awe inspiring.

My ever changing local walk carries me year by year through the seasons. The edges of the larger reservoir are profuse with buttercups, soapwort and spotted orchids in the summer. Autumn sees the woods a blaze of browns and reds, with hawthorn berries, elderberries and hips and haws colouring the hedgerows. In winter my stroll can become a major expedition, on one occasion with snowdrifts up to six feet deep whipped by the wind into weird and wonderful shapes. It then seems a miracle how the lambs, the daffodils and the cowslips will ever appear again, and that the martins and swallows will return. But they do. Thus through this commonplace round I find the evidence of God, who is not only the Creator, but the Sustainer of creation this year, next year and throughout eternity.

We have two children, Peter and Kirsten. I take it for granted now that they are persons in their own right. But at quite unexpected moments over the years, when pushing the pram out, seeing them depart for their first day at school, at the meal table, in the middle of a game of football, gazing at them when they were asleep, sharing my local walk with them, watching them get their degrees, I have been startled by the realization that these are human beings whom I have helped to create. It is an experience as old as the hills, yet for me it is no less amazing for that. Often with that moment of awakening to the marvel of human life has come a deep sense of awe that children are a gift so incredible that only a God of life and love could be the giver.

> You deny the existence of God?
> Look forth on those forest-clothed hills,
> Hark to the song of the birds,
> Gaze up at the stars in the night,
> Hear the call of the children at play.
>
> Why, the world is resplendent with God:
> His glory cannot be veiled:
> Through the garment of matter it shines,
> As the sun through a curtain of cloud.
>
> Man needs but the listening ear,
> But the eye that is willing to see:
> With these he shall know and be glad
> In the living assurance of God.[1]

So writes John Hoyland, the Quaker missionary and one of my spiritual heroes.

My experiences of God as the Creator and Sustainer of all things and all people have brought a deep sense of thanksgiving. This does not mean I can forget the reality of evil. It means that in spite of darkness and death, and the bewilderment I often experience in their presence, I am able to celebrate the fact that the cosmos is ultimately in the hands of a loving Creator seeking the fulfilment and perfection of his creation.

This conviction has been more than mine. It has been at the heart of the religious experience of some of the most down-to-earth men and women in history – the psalmist for one. Despite his constant encounter with cruelty and hatred, he still believed that a God of steadfast love governed the universe and that all things – sun, moon, stars; the sea and the sky; fire and hail; snow and frost; mountains and hills; animals and birds; as well as "kings of the earth and all peoples, princes and all rulers of the earth. Young men and maidens together, old men and children" should "praise the name of the Lord, for his name alone is exalted; his glory is above earth and heaven."[2]

Nor has such an offering of praise been a matter only for the sanctuary. The psalmist certainly worshipped there. But he met and responded thankfully to God wherever the exchange between human and divine life took place. Another of my spiritual heroes is Edward Wilson, the Antarctic explorer. He had a profound Christian faith and constant sense of the presence of God. This was nourished not so much by church worship, which he often found claustrophobic and deadening, but by his passion for the beauty of the natural world; observing it, exploring it, studying it, painting it, but often simply being still and encountering God within it.

Nor was it only in wild and remote places that Wilson was drawn to worship. After watching, from his rooms in

Battersea, a sunset which momentarily transfigured "all the smoke and dust and dirt and squalor, and miles of chimney-pots and spires and turrets, the Big Wheel and searchlight tower of Earls' Court, steamers and tugs and barges and deep red sails", he wrote how it brought home to him "that the whole big mixture of dirt and cleanliness, right and wrong, ugliness and beauty, love and self-denial and meanness and fear – the whole bag of tricks – is under one law of life, the law of sure and slow development into the perfected love of God."[3]

Such experiences, mine as well as those of others, convince me that we cannot allow anyone or anything less than God to become the focus of our praise and worship. They convince me, too, that he must be acknowledged and worshipped as "the Lord and Giver of life" wherever and whenever we encounter him. This means that we must give thanks for the achievements of science and technology, industry and commerce, as well as the glory of earth, sea and sky. But it must be thanks first and foremost to God, not to man or woman. The pyramid and the skyscraper point upwards as well as downwards. The computer reveals the wonder of God's gift of intelligence and memory, and not just the brilliance of human minds.

One of the crises of our time is that materialism and consumerism threaten to usurp the place of God the Creator and Preserver. These experiences warn us that we dare not idolize well-being or the means by which it is attained. To make a God of consumer goods, of market forces or of the planned economy, is to cut ourselves off from the very source of life and sustenance.

If these encounters with God the Creator call us first and foremost to worship him, and him alone, wherever we meet him, they also indicate that we are meant to be co-workers with him, stewards of this planet and its resources.

There is an increasingly important struggle to be engaged in here. My local walk will probably survive a few years longer. But I can now see across the valley the great ugly scar of the cutting for the new M42 which will soon channel a vast quantity of traffic, with the accompanying noise and exhaust fumes, through this attractive and relatively quiet bit of the countryside. A Swiss friend of ours was recently speaking of the growing concern of countries such as hers over the devastation to woods and forest caused by acid rain. And as if to underline this point with a vengeance, there is before me as I write one of many daily papers covered with article after article about the explosion at the Chernobyl nuclear reactor.

Yet even this last example of our failure to be effective stewards of God's creation pales into insignificance when compared with the sight of the mushroom cloud towering over the landscape. Not so long ago I saw an American film called *The Day After*, which recounted the imaginary story of a town in the southern states immediately following the dropping of an atomic bomb. A short time later I happened to be out on my local walk, and for a moment saw in my mind's eye that landscape blasted, burnt, then frozen and dying as the result of nuclear war. I grasped with agonizing vividness that the total annihilation of life was no passing nightmare but a real and immediate possibility. It was an horrific vision to set against my many experiences of a planet transformed by the touch of the divine into a foretaste of eternity.

There are no easy answers to the life or death crises we face. But I believe that it matters immensely from where we draw our inspiration, and where we start our journey in pursuit of the health and wholeness of our planet. If that journey begins with us it will end with us; and there is no hope. If it begins with God the Creator, there is light upon the horizon.

Thus any act of worship through which we receive the grace of God and in return offer our lives to him, in short any true sacrament, must somehow embrace the gift of creation and our commission to be its stewards. This exchange of life is well expressed by Geoffrey Studdert-Kennedy in a hymn which first came alive for me when sung on a brilliantly sunny morning at Willersley Castle, a Methodist Guild guest house in Derbyshire:

> Awake, awake to love and work,
> The lark is in the sky,
> The fields are wet with diamond dew,
> The worlds awake to cry
> Their blessings on the Lord of Life,
> As he goes meekly by.
>
> Come, let thy voice be one with theirs,
> Shout with their shout of praise;
> See how the giant sun soars up,
> Great lord of years and days!
> So let the love of Jesus come,
> And set thy soul ablaze.
>
> To give and give, and give again,
> What God hath given thee;
> To spend thy self nor count the cost,
> To serve right gloriously
> The God who gave all words that are,
> And all that are to be.[4]

I find an understanding of sacrament, as embracing the gift of creation and our stewardship of it, evident in an even more profound way in the writings of Teilhard de Chardin, the French palaeontologist and Jesuit priest. In *The Mass on the World* he writes:

Since once again, Lord – though this time not in the forests of the Aisne but in the steppes of Asia – I have neither bread, nor wine, nor altar, I will raise myself beyond these symbols, up to the pure majesty of the real itself; I, your priest, will make the whole earth my altar and on it will offer you all the labours and sufferings of the world.

Over there, on the horizon, the sun has just touched with light the outermost fringe of the eastern sky. Once again, beneath this moving sheet of fire, the living surface of the earth wakes and trembles, and once again begins its fearful travail. I will place on my paten, O God, the harvest to be won by this renewal of labour. Into my chalice I shall pour all the sap which is to be pressed out this day from the earth's fruits.[5]

All of us are called to be members of this priesthood, and to share in the sacrament of creation through which God offers us life and we in turn offer it back to him in praise and thanksgiving.

2. The Liberator

I have been frightened many times when mountaineering but rarely more so than when, as a fifteen-year-old, I was lost on the slopes of the Crib Goch, the jagged ridge offering one of the more testing routes up Snowdon. Our small party had become well spread out in taking an unpathed and dangerous short cut up to the ridge, when suddenly a heavy mist enveloped us. I could see and hear nobody. I was a young and inexperienced climber, lost and alone in a grey and formidable wilderness of rock and scree. For the first time on the hills I knew real panic. And in that moment I felt the numbing loneliness of this planet when one seems bereft of fellow human beings.

To be "alive" in an impersonal, unfeeling and uncaring universe, however beautiful or majestic, would be hell. I am only moved by the glory of the dawn over the Jotunheimen mountains, the mysterious joy of the spring, or the wonder of the changing seasons, because they enable me to exchange life with another person, to enter into a living relationship with someone as real as myself. Awe and wonder, joy and peace, only come to me through creation because time and again I have encountered a living and loving Creator. When his presence has been most intense I have felt alive and fulfilled; when it has been distant I have felt lost and afraid.

This sense of the presence of a personal God has been with me as long as I can remember. Like any relationship it has changed and developed, had its peaks and its troughs, but, I dare to hope, it has also "matured" over the years. At fourteen, one of the earliest of those experiences was a sense of falling deeply in love with God, as I sat for an hour or more on the edge of Derwent Water watching the lake in front and Skiddaw beyond turning crimson in the light of the setting sun.

But what was this Creator really like? He might reveal something of himself through the natural world, but how could he be recognized away from lakes and hills and forests and streams? The answer which eventually came to me was that he could be discovered through ordinary people made extraordinary by his love. I discovered that this living God transformed not only the physical world around me but men and women as well.

Many, many people have shown me something of what God is like. Here I mention only two: my mother and my father.

My mother was a deeply caring person, not only for her children and her own parents (she looked after my grandmother, who lived with us for over fifteen years, with immense dedication), but for any who came her way. She constantly visited and helped neighbours and friends, as well as the many who passed through her Methodist Sunday

School class and later her adult group. She was a sensitive and gentle woman to whom angry words were unknown. As an avid reader she wholeheartedly opened herself to the experiences of other people and to new ideas: at seventy I recall her deciding to introduce the members of her women's meeting to the ideas of John Robinson in *Honest to God*!

My father is now nearly ninety. I have met few people with such a zest for living. He still gardens, goes to Kwiksave and drives a car. He is a very good amateur artist and a keen bird watcher. Only a few years ago he visited a friend in South Africa for a six-week stay and thoroughly enjoyed the trip. He is a person of great insight and wisdom, born out of twenty years as the first personnel manager appointed by Boots the Chemist, and long service as a marriage guidance counsellor, amongst other experiences. Until retirement he gave himself wholeheartedly to his young people's group at the local church, some of whom still call to see him. He has a deep sense of loyalty, not least to the Methodist Church, which has seen him worshipping twice a Sunday for as long as I can remember.

These bare facts convey little of my parents' constant, yet often unconscious, witness to a loving God and to his presence permeating every aspect of their daily lives. It was not a fusty faith, but one which was always open to new discoveries and fresh truths. There was questioning and honest doubt. But beneath our many family discussions of life and religion lay their quiet assurance that God was utterly real and vitally alive.

For my mother, faith was a deeply person-centred affair; for my father, steeped in the writing of Evelyn Underhill, it was more of a mystical experience, though tempered by a mischievous sense of fun in which I often delighted as a child. As I grew, I found myself to be loved fully and completely, and knew that this affirmation of me as a person, faults as well as strengths, was grounded in my parents' own experience of God's unfailing love for them. Helped by their faith, which enriched both our relationships as a family and our home life, and shaped our attitudes to the world beyond, I was gradually able to make the connection between the God of sunsets and dawns, of hills and streams, of the changing seasons, and the world of ordinary people.

This was also because my parents' "Yes" to life and "Yes" to God, as well as "Yes" to me, focused on and continually directed my attention to a real person, Jesus Christ; one whom they were convinced had demonstrated and still uniquely did demonstrate the nature and the purposes of God for humankind.

They believed that God working in and through this Jesus Christ, whose spirit was alive and active in the world, had given them a totally trustworthy guide for their journey through life. So I was taken without fail on the mile walk each week to morning worship at our local Methodist Church in Beeston, Nottingham, and I listened to a constant round of Bible stories every Sunday afternoon at Sunday School. It was for me an often dull part of our family routine. But through it all I gradually became familiar with the life and teachings of Christ.

I had begun to realize that if God the Creator was to fulfil his early promise, then somehow he had to earth himself in a way which had meaning for everyday life. I slowly came to believe that in no human being could I see this as more likely to have happened than in the person of Jesus Christ. Even more compelling, I began to sense this figure breaking free from the often remote language of sermon, hymnbook and Bible, and accompanying me in person over the hills, by the side of the lakes and through the valleys. I slowly came to feel that my "Yes" to God had at some point to become a "Yes" to Christ as well.

I have had in my Bible for many years a picture by Herbert Beecroft which portrays the face of Christ turning to look at Peter as the latter denies him. As I became more aware of the call of Christ to follow him in order to fulfil my own human possibilities, I became increasingly aware of my failures and lack of resources. I began to understand that to say "Yes" to Christ meant not only being affirmed and encouraged, but being called to account. His love was unconditional. Yet it was also conditional, because there were rules of the road which had to be learnt if the journey were to be undertaken and to progress successfully.

At fifteen I was converted at a Monday evening rally at my home church in Beeston. What decided me to go forward was not just an appeal for commitment made by Bill Gowland, then Methodist minister of the Albert Hall, Manchester, but a deep yearning to live my life as fully as possible for Christ. It was a wish to be rid of self-centredness and self-indulgence, as well as a desire to follow the example of Bill Gowland in his ministry to the down-and-outs on the Manchester streets. I wanted to be liberated from the meanderings of the past, and to follow Christ, whose service, it was said, was perfect freedom.

In some ways my conversion was the end of a stage of a journey I had begun without realizing it. I did not want so much to begin again as to make a better job of the future. I not only felt "saved" from the failures of the past and the guilt that went with it, though that was important enough, but liberated to live, and to help others to live, a more Christ-centred life. It was a choice I made openly and freely. Despite all the later rationalizations which tempt one to dismiss such events as adolescent romanticism, it was for me a major turning point on the journey.

On the window ledge of my office at Westhill College in Birmingham is a small segment of wood chipped off a pine tree. It is now dry, brittle and dusty, with the bark peeling off. Along with the other bric-à-brac on the same sill, it is no doubt regarded by the cleaner as fit only for the dustbin. But it reminds me of another important moment of liberation.

The piece of pine came from a wood near Gomshall, in Surrey, through which I was walking on a misty April morning in 1961. It was one of the many splinters littering the ground as a result of recent felling and trimming by the Forestry Commission. I picked it up because the vivid maroon colouring of the rain-soaked chippings, the rich scent of the oozing resin and the mysterious beauty of the still spring morning had suddenly brought me to life again after the numbing experience of a long and serious nervous breakdown. I felt in that moment something of what I imagine Mary must have felt on another spring morning two thousand years ago when Christ spoke her name.

Nearly three years before my walk in the Surrey woods, my finals at Oxford, accompanied by a number of other draining events, had led to nervous exhaustion and eventual collapse. Inept medical treatment had made matters worse. I was left sleepless, afraid, depressed, sensually drained, and at times captive within a world of grim forebodings. Yet throughout this confusing and distressing period of my life I was as ever made aware of the affirming love of God in Christ through family and friends. My parents and Sue, now my wife, sustained and supported me along this tough stretch of the journey in many Christ-like ways. So too did others, one the Jewish lady whom I have already mentioned, who claimed no formal Christian commitment.

This nervous breakdown brought other unexpected gains. I reached a greater awareness of who I was and, perhaps more to the point, who I was not. I felt that in some strange way I was being called to account again because of my failure to accept the real me. I came to see that my breakdown was in part the consequence of unrealistic ambitions and an interpretation of my "vocation" which was far more self- than Christ-centred.

Yet through it all, the door to Christ's liberating and renewing grace remained open. It was this life-giving energy, this resurrection power, which burst into my consciousness with such overwhelming force in the Surrey woods. With that experience came a recognition that even the hell of the last few years might also be counted as an important part of the journey towards "mature manhood, measured by nothing less than the full stature of Christ."[6]

But we are all human beings. We soon forget or deny our liberation. By the time I was forty other circumstances were again threatening to choke my "Yes" to life.

In the late 'sixties I had undertaken a doctorate in sociology at Sheffield University. My commitment to the insights of sociological analysis brought a growing scepticism about religious experience, my own included, and cynicism about virtually all things ecclesiastical. My honest doubts were often overtaken by naïve rationalism, and considerable scorn of much for which the church seemed to stand.

At the same time life appeared to be closing in physically as well as spiritually. Liberation from a good deal of sexual guilt as an adolescent had not freed me as an adult to know how to use and express sexuality creatively. I was still living in the past, tied to traditions and taboos the validity of which I had neither dared to test out nor to accept genuinely as my own. Accompanying these sexual frustrations, I experienced a series of aggravating physical ailments which necessitated half a dozen periods of hospital treatment and, much worse as far as I was concerned, called into question my ability to go climbing mountains or even walking again.

It was a crisis which led to many upheavals, personal and domestic, as well as to much questioning of my vocation as an ordained minister. I experienced a sense of life passing me by, obsessional anxieties over health and strength, and a general loss of nerve. My relationships were for a while in turmoil, with great "highs" and deep "lows", and I travelled up numerous cul-de-sacs in pursuit of what I felt would provide fulfilment. Disappointment and anger with a church which seemed to be oblivious to its steady decline was one more factor which eventually led me to a move from Methodist circuit work to a college of education.

Yet somehow I knew that through it all Christ was still around, watching, waiting and inviting me to take stock in the light of his purposes for me. As before, his affirmation of me, his raising my awareness to the potential of my own life, and his calling me to account, were mediated through many people far more aware of his ways than I was. Liberation and renewal came again, though this time more as a gradual re-awakening than a dramatic happening. Amongst others who set me on my way were the Roman Catholic La Retraite Sisters and the Sisters of Charity of St Paul, who confirmed me in my conviction that Christ is no respecter of denominational boundaries.

So I come to the present time, still carrying with me many of the weaknesses, confusions and fears which have knocked me off course in the past. I am still learning to appreciate that which remains very much my shadow, and discovering how to use its power in creative rather than destructive ways. Yet I remain as certain as I can be that Christ continues to walk alongside me, affirming me, rousing me to make the utmost of my life, calling me to account, offering me a free choice in working out my own salvation, and liberating me time and time again to pursue the journey towards becoming the fully human person he wishes me to be.

My hope is summed up in a hymn of Charles Wesley's which I have always sung with great fervour, but the deeper meaning of which I have only slowly come to grasp:

> Love divine, all loves excelling,
> Joy of heaven, to earth come down;
> Fix in us Thy humble dwelling,
> All Thy faithful mercies crown:
> Jesu, Thou art all compassion,
> Pure unbounded love Thou art;
> Visit us with Thy salvation,
> Enter every trembling heart.

Come, almighty to deliver,
Let us all Thy grace receive;
Suddenly return, and never,
Never more Thy temples leave:
Thee we would be always blessing,
Serve Thee as Thy hosts above,
Pray, and praise Thee, without ceasing,
Glory in Thy perfect love.

Finish then Thy new creation,
Pure and spotless let us be;
Let us see Thy great salvation,
Perfectly restored in Thee;
Changed from glory into glory,
Till in heaven we take our place,
Till we cast our crowns before Thee,
Lost in wonder, love and praise.[7]

I know that the gift of liberation in Christ which I have experienced cannot be hugged to myself. I have only discovered it and been able to receive it because many people have been channels of his divine grace. My own integrity is called into question if I do not attempt to love and to liberate as I have been loved and liberated. The same is true, I believe, for all of us who call ourselves Christians.

Each and every person is unique and of infinite value in the eyes of God the Creator and Christ the Liberator. But it is a message of affirmation that must be offered first to those who are devalued and hopeless. "Go and tell John what you have seen and heard", Christ said to his questioners. "The blind receive their sight, the lame walk, lepers are cleansed, and the deaf hear, the dead are raised up, the poor have good news preached to them."[8]

For me, the deprivation and violence of Handsworth, Birmingham, symbolizes something of the challenge which church and society face in this connection. For over a decade my community and youth work students from Westhill College have had practical work placements in the area, giving me the opportunity to visit Handsworth regularly and talk to many of those living and working there.

Affirmation, personal, social, economic and political, is desperately needed in such a neighbourhood where fulltime work is an increasingly precious commodity. In the locality where the riots took place in September 1985, male unemployment was 46 per cent.[9] It remains a situation which leads to a host of destructive emotions – apathy, despair, anger and hatred – with consequent violence, domestic and public. Without affirmation there is no hope, without hope there is no vision of community, without a vision the people perish.

For those between fifteen and eighteen years old the unemployment rate in the riot-torn part of Handsworth was 54 per cent, though many schools put it a great deal higher. Most of these young people are black and of West Indian or Asian parentage. Not only do they remain unaffirmed, but unaware of their potential as adults in the making. We now know that though there are many good teachers in such areas, our education system as a whole undervalues black pupils and fails to raise their awareness to their own academic capabilities.[10] Such young people often fall by the way because they come to accept a low assessment of their own potential and then live up (or down) to that.

Pauline, Keith and Lehona were black students from Handsworth who came to Westhill College to train as community and youth workers. They had somehow found affirmation in the midst of deprivation, they had somehow come to a realization of their own skills and human potential. But that was not enough. If genuine liberation is to come, we have to be called to account, test out our strengths and weaknesses for the journey ahead, prove ourselves as committed and obtain the resources needed for that undertaking. In this sense to be called to account affirms us and raises our awareness.

Pauline, Keith and Lehona are now qualified. Pauline and Lehona are employed in social work, and Keith is a youth officer. They are thus free to enrich their experience, develop their own talents further and, in their turn, to offer liberation to others who are disadvantaged and marginalized. For Lehona, a keen member of a black church in Handsworth, such a calling is undoubtedly Christ-centred. But for Pauline and Keith his name does not enter the picture. Does it matter?

I do not believe so – at least at this stage of the journey. Those that are not against him are for him. Those who seek to liberate others are themselves on the way to liberation and fulfilment. If that journey is faithfully pursued then, whatever our starting point, we cannot help but reflect his purposes and converge on his kingdom.

I fear more for the self-sufficient and the privileged. It is so often they, amongst whose number we as Christians are usually found, who condone deprivation, who fail to offer the disadvantaged any hope of realizing their human potential, and who do not allow the poor the opportunity of autonomy. To fail to minister to the hungry, the thirsty, the stranger, the naked, the sick and the prisoner,[11] is to fail to minister to Christ himself. Such failure leads not to liberation but to captivity for all.

3. The Unifier

One of the most vivid memories of my youth was the immensely enjoyable Saturday evening socials held at my home church. They were masterpieces of organization with games galore, a few old-time dances thrown in (not too many, as dancing was still suspect for Methodists) and, as I saw them, scrumptious refreshments. Such occasions did more to teach me about Christian fellowship than scores of Sunday services.

There were other means of Christian fellowship which came my way at Beeston. In my 'teen years the Wesley Guild was one of the most important of these. The Guild was an all-age Methodist association founded late in the nineteenth century and "based on personal commitment to Christ as the Lord of all good life".[12] Its motto was "One heart, one way". Its aims were traditionally expressed in "the four C's" – comradeship, culture, Christian services and consecration – and the pattern of its week night meetings followed each of these themes in turn.

For me, the "C" which the Guild brought as vividly to life as any was comradeship. I experienced a real depth of Christian fellowship in the Guild evenings I attended regularly, as well as in outings of a serving or social nature. I was thrilled to go on one occasion as a representative from Nottingham to the national Wesley Guild conference in Liverpool, where I made my maiden speech in a major church assembly.

I also found a strong sense of comradeship at Wesley Guild guest houses such as Willersley Castle, near Matlock, where I went for numerous conferences. I spent the second year of my national service on a remote army camp near Grange-over-Sands, south of the Lake District, during which time Abbots Hall, the Guild holiday centre just outside Grange, became a much appreciated support group; a home base made all the more welcoming by the generous hospitality of its caretaker and his family.

These early experiences within Methodism introduced me to what I would now call "the fellowship of the Holy Spirit". I came to experience the Christian life not just as an encounter with God the Creator, nor simply as a personal journey with Christ towards freedom and integrity, but as a corporate expedition made possible through the companionship of fellow travellers.

As the years passed, this sense of Christian solidarity became one of ever increasing circles. At Oxford Univesity, where I went after national service, it was a John Wesley Society group which sustained and englarged my faith. A dozen or more of us gathered every Sunday afternoon during term-time for discussion, prayers and of course tea, as well as participating in numerous social outings. Though we greatly enjoyed ourselves, we also supported one another through traumas that ranged from broken romances to failed exams, from crises of faith to problems with the law. On two occasions the group travelled down to the Methodist Mission in Bermondsey to spend a week of the vacation visiting the council flats in the vicinity, offering the services of the Mission to many in the area in acute economic or social need. The old close-knit extended family life of Bermondsey had by this time all but collapsed, leaving a neighbourhood in which isolation and loneliness were rife. Thus these visits also introduced me to the need for economic justice, support and caring within the inner city.

The John Wesley group at Oxford deepened and widened my understanding of the fellowship of the Holy Spirit in a way that left a lasting impression. Many of its members have remained my friends, even though contact has been limited by changing circumstances. One of the group, Sue, I fell in love with and married. Group members came from several other churches besides Methodism, and one or two would not have claimed the name Christian. Yet somehow all of us, though very different people, experienced a powerful sense of belonging.

The boundaries of Christian fellowship have gone on widening for me ever since. For four of the six years I spent as the Methodist minister in West Greenwich, immediately following my ministry in Woodhouse, I was part of the first shared Presbyterian/Methodist church in England. The Methodist church to which I had originally been posted proved to be on the point of collapse, so we closed our doors and, despite some strident local opposition, moved across the road to join up with St Mark's, South Street.

We were given a marvellous reception by the Presbyterian congregation, made to feel fully members of the united church, and soon began to regard St Mark's as our home. I gained a great deal from the partnership with David Gardner, my Presbyterian colleague, and learnt to appreciate the traditions and ethos of his denomination in a way that would otherwise have been impossible. Despite the difficulties and disappointments which came our way, not least in the limited impact our united venture made on the neighbourhood as a whole, the experience gave me further insight into the meaning of the unity of the Holy Spirit.

In 1983, I found myself worshipping in a very different kind of Christian assembly. It was something which, though of much shorter duration, has remained another peak experience of my life. I was with five thousand people, from over a hundred different countries and two hundred and fifty churches, gathered in the Pacific Coliseum, Vancouver, for the opening ceremony of the Sixth Assembly of the World Council of Churches. The two and a half weeks of this great international event, the first I had attended, were made especially memorable by the constant reminders of the deep sense of unity encompassing amazing diversity. Every day brought new encounters. One morning over breakfast I chatted to a Baptist layman from Moscow, in the assembly hall I sat beside a German Lutheran woman pastor, I ate lunch with a black community worker from Cape Town, and spent the evening with a Methodist minister from the United States.

The Assembly itself provided many signs of togetherness, all playing their part in one of the great symbols of Christian unity in our world today. There were the many visitors from far and near, including members of local churches in the Vancouver area. The latter gave hospitality to delegates before and after the event as well as at the weekends during

it. I enjoyed a visit to a Christian family of very modest
means, who shared their home and table and then drove me
out in their battered old car to see some of the glorious
scenery of British Columbia. The thoughtfulness of the
Canadian people was also in evidence at our registration for
the Assembly itself. We received a canvas holdall in which
to carry our papers, each bag having been made by local
residents and containing a letter of welcome.

Another sign of fellowship was offered by three public
meeting places located on the campus of the University of
British Columbia, where the Assembly was held. One was
"The Ploughshares Coffee House" where discussions about
justice and peace issues took place; a second was "The
Well", a centre staffed by women to promote talks and
events relating to women's issues; a third was an "Interfaith
Centre" set up for dialogue between those belonging to the
different major world religions. These centres were regarded as an integral part of the Assembly and, though
having no formal voice in its proceedings, provided an
invaluable meeting point for many.

The Assembly as such was another sign of unity. The
sight of the eight hundred delegates in session always impressed me. From the gallery of the huge gymnasium where
the Assembly met, I could see the names of countries on the
rows of tables below, indicating a great geographical spread.
At times I marvelled that the Christian faith had crossed so
many barriers, physical and cultural, to make possible this
witness to the diversity yet unity of the church. Evidence of
continuing divisions was still there: Roman Catholics being
present only as "observers", members of the Salvation
Army being unhappy about too much reference to justice
and too little to evangelism, and militant conservative
evangelicals claiming on placards that the World Council of
Churches was in the hands of the K.G.B. But all this was
nothing compared with the living, dynamic and widespread
sense of solidarity manifest throughout the fortnight.

At the heart of these signs of fellowship was worship, held in a great tent erected specially for that purpose. Every day, song, music, dance and drama from different continents were used in a way that enriched the sense of belonging to a worldwide church. This was powerfully symbolized by our saying of the Lord's Prayer together in some thirty different languages. At the concluding act of worship hundreds of small pictures of people were pinned to the walls of the tent. The drawings were done by children of many countries, the back of each bearing a name and address of the young artist for delegates to write to in acknowledgement. The final act of worship of the Assembly ended with a massive multi-national conga.

The theme of the Sixth Assembly was "Jesus Christ, the Life of the world". The slogan on the Assembly T-shirts read "Choose Life". And the formal message of the delegates to churches throughout the world was headed "Life Together". My visit to Vancouver gave me a brief but impressive glimpse of what life together in the unity of the Spirit could be like.

Even so, the reality of the difficult journey to unity also broke in on us at Vancouver. Through the gift of a huge totem pole, as well as by speeches and drama, the Assembly was introduced to the plight of the Canadian Indians, struggling to retain their economic independence and cultural identity. During the Assembly, riots erupted in Sri Lanka and a number of delegates from that part of the world had to hurry back home.

For me, however, the continuing challenge of a divided and suffering world was presented most poignantly in the plea for justice and reconciliation in South Africa made by Desmond Tutu to delegates and visitors packed into the Assembly's main hall. This struck a personal chord, because only twelve months before Sue and I had spent five weeks in South Africa exploring the social and political situation there. It was a short but unforgettable experience, which reminded me how imperative it was for all of us who have been privileged to know something of the unity of the Holy Spirit to strive so that all can share it.

Man's failure in South Africa to see that even the most basic of human rights are met reveals the strength of the forces of disunity at work in our world. These powers of darkness are seen only too vividly in the appalling poverty of the homelands. The human degradation there was brought home on one of our visits by the sight of a young boy and his sick mother living in a broken down hut with a leaking tin roof, and possessing no furniture but two ramshackle beds, a rickety table and an old stove. The father and husband worked far away seeking to scrape a little money together to send to his family. We also witnessed the divisive consequences of apartheid, epitomized by the vast township of Soweto, separated from Johannesburg by well policed arterial roads and a barren no-man's-land, to which all blacks of whatever social standing have to return after their day's work in the city. All are treated as third-class citizens in a host of ways, from restricted use of the public transport system and toilets to lack of educational and political rights.

Yet many other societies besides South Africa need to discover the unity of the Spirit, to experience healing and wholeness. Britain itself is increasingly becoming "two nations", with the rich growing richer and the poor poorer, as anyone travelling by train from Glasgow to London can see. And a stone's throw across the water lies Northern Ireland, with confrontation and conflict even more starkly in evidence.

Evil within nations operates as destructively as within individuals. There can be no unity without reconciliation, and no reconciliation without justice. But my experiences from Beeston to Vancouver, from Bermondsey to Soweto, persuade me that without a vision of unity, and without the power of the Holy Spirit the Unifier to enable that vision to become reality, there is no hope of glory for our world.

4. The Kingdom Community

The end of our journeying is the fulfilment of all that our planet, of each person and every society have it in them to be. Our quest for the health and wholeness of the planet has its origins in the purposes of God the Creator of life and beauty. Our search for personal autonomy and fulfilment is a response to the call of Christ the Liberator. Our desire for the unity of humankind, be that within the small group or between nations, comes from the Holy Spirit the Unifier.

My own experiences have led me to a deep sense of an exchange of life with God as Creator, a "human" Companion accompanying me on the journey, or a dynamic Spirit. At other times these three sources of life have merged into one vibrant whole. When this has happened, I believe they have revealed to me something of what Christians call the Holy Trinity, God in three Persons yet one God, the ultimate source and fulfilment of all things.

If this is the case, what light does it throw on the purpose of our journey? In the previous chapter I summed up the supreme human quest as the search for community, in the deepest and most all-embracing sense of that term. I call our divine vocation, to which our human destiny is intimately related, the search for the kingdom community.

In the New Testament the kingdom is associated more with the sovereignty than with the people of God. But at that time the latter had still to be called into being. Once done, through the ministry of Christ and by the preaching of the apostles, the kingdom as a community became a theological and sociological reality on earth as in heaven.

The kingdom community is the consummation of the divine life within all things. It is the fulfilment of the divine potential of planet, persons and people, separately and together. It is what we are wholly meant to be. It is both a divine undertaking and a human project. It is a community that is already in being, yet is for ever becoming.

When I was a 'teenager I sang with great verve a hymn of James Small, the third verse of which goes as follows:

> I've found a Friend; O such a Friend!
> All power to him is given,
> To guard me on my onward course
> And bring me safe to heaven.
> Eternal glories gleam afar,
> To nerve my faint endeavour;
> So now to watch, to work, to war,
> And then to rest for ever.[13]

I can now imagine nothing worse, and I hope less like heaven, than having "to rest for ever". I see the building of human community as a never ending process because so, too, is the creation of the kingdom community. If we are open to encounter with the Trinity we never cease being changed "from glory into glory" for heaven is not a "place", but "a moving web" of loving relationships founded on an eternal exchange of life.

At the heart of the kingdom community lies the divine as well as human "Yes" to life, and "Yes" to life together. If the Trinity is seen in this context, then it is not a static symbol but an attempt to describe the intimate interdependence of three Persons. The encounter and exchange between Father, Son and Holy Spirit must always have been, and always will be, ongoing, or it can never have been a reality. We are engaged in an exchange of life because God is too; we are involved in a process of becoming as well as being because, in some profound and life-giving way, God is as well.

This continuing exchange of divine life with divine life, of divine life with human life, and of human life with human life, means that the kingdom community is characterized by the sharing of all we are and all we have. This involves a sharing of love. But the Trinity also represents the sharing of power and authority. Father, Son and Holy Spirit have different but equally important "rights" and responsibilities. So it is with the kingdom community. So it must be with our world if its potential is to be realized.

On the presence of the kingdom community rests the fulfilment or failure of all human ambitions to build or sustain community. I have in this chapter touched on some of the consequences of our saying "No" to life and "No" to life together. To reject or ignore the kingdom community, its vitality, its power of regeneration and renewal, its energy, is to court the extinction of our planet, to deny men and women liberation and to condemn humankind to fragmentation. There will be no end to pollution or the threat of nuclear catastrophe, no liberation of the physically, mentally or socially vulnerable, no diminution of injustice and oppression, until the values of the kingdom community, and their divine source, are honoured for what they are. "You shall have no other gods before me"[14] is as true a requirement for the building of an enduring community in our generation as it was for the Children of Israel in search of the promised land many centuries ago.

Their journey was a long and arduous one. It required commitment to the divine purpose and courage to live it out in practice. But in return God gave his word that he would support them on the way, and that their hopes would eventually be fulfilled. It was a covenant which sums up the crucial fact that our journey is a partnership in which God and man and woman are fellow travellers.

The annual covenant service of my own Methodist Church has always been a vivid reminder for me of the amazing offer of this partnership "for life". It is a service held at the beginning of each year. It brings to remembrance "God's promise that he will fulfil, in and through us, all that he declared in Jesus Christ" and that in response "we stand pledged to live no more unto ourselves, but to him who loved us and gave himself for us".[15] Acts of adoration, thanksgiving and confession are followed by the act of covenanting itself. This culminates in the great affirmation:

> And now, O glorious and blessed God, Father, Son and Holy Spirit, Thou art mine and I am thine. So be it. And the covenant which I have made on earth, let it be ratified in heaven.

Year after year this service declares that our hope of glory rests on the fact that God is ours and we are his; that the search for the kingdom community cannot fail if we respond to the offer of his life, love and power given to the people of Israel on Mount Sinai, renewed by his Son in the upper room before his crucifixion and, thenceforth, made available through his Spirit to all people at all times.

The new covenant points to the fact that the journey towards the kingdom community is costly, even more so for God than for us. He is no aloof deity shouting directions from on high. The Trinity describes a God who in Christ lived and suffered and died as one with us, so that by his resurrection the power of evil and death could be broken for ever, and liberation be offered to the whole creation. As the properties of each Person of the Trinity belong to all, so does the pain and suffering caused by life refused and love rejected. Thus the cost of creating, of liberating and of uniting are all seen in the passion of Christ. Yet because of that costly divine commitment to the kingdom community the journey is now made possible for each and every person who wants to set out on it. We can begin, whoever we are, wherever we are and whenever we wish.

5. Beginning the Search

For some people the search for the kingdom community is given meaning by a deep concern for the conservation and good stewardship of the resources, aesthetic and material, of our planet. Some see the journey in terms of personal growth and fulfilment. Others are motivated by a passion for social justice and a fairer distribution of wealth. All are legitimate points of departure.

What matters is not where we begin, but widening our horizons and our understanding of the whole of the kingdom community as we travel. We have to learn that our journey at some stage must embrace the sustaining of life on earth, the autonomy of the individual and the unity of the world, all three. For the kingdom community to come, each and every one of us has eventually to make a response which furthers the potential of the whole and not just of one part.

For a few the search for the kingdom community will begin at an international level and focus on the relations between the major political powers. For most of us it will start at a more modest level – the city, the town, the neighbourhood, the home. It does not matter where this journey begins as long as there is a growing awareness that both the macro and micro dimensions of human life have a complementary role to play in the coming of the kingdom. To save our souls and lose the world is no better than saving the world and losing our souls.

For me "home ground" has always been an important arena in which to learn about the kingdom community. Sue and I have now been married for twenty-five years, a partnership which began in a Methodist church in Bradford with a mutual commitment before God – our covenant – to share with him the journey of life.

It was an amazing privilege to be able to be partners, through the birth of Peter and Kirsten, in God's creative activity. Their arrival brought home to us the preciousness as well as the wonder of life. Only a few hours after Kirsten was born we were informed that she faced an immediate major operation of long duration. We were suddenly made vividly aware of God not only as Creator but as Preserver of humankind. I remember being alone with Kirsten for a few moments before her surgery, quietly baptizing her, in the conviction that whatever happened all was somehow well. I went into a nearby church to pray and, though being faced with the possible ending of a human life, was never more sure of its eternal nature. Kirsten survived the operation and, despite almost six months' hospitalization, with daily reports varying from the most pessimistic to the most reassuring, eventually came home for good. We were launched into the serious business of enabling two energetic children to make the most of their lives.

Since then our home has been a continuing and energetic exchange of life. I hope that Sue and I have enabled Peter and Kirsten to experience something of the life in us. Through Sue they have, I believe, caught a feel of the riches of music and, through me, a glimpse of the beauty of nature. We have helped them face some of the more testing experiences of their school years, and seen them through university. We have, not too gently, pushed them out into a wider world, welcoming the chances that have come for them to visit Europe, the Middle East and the United States. We have shared with them our different approaches to faith and religion and hope that, in their own way, they may have been awakened to the meaning of life, liberation and unity.

Sue has helped Peter and Kirsten to see that life is a continuing journey towards fulfilment. Her early career in music failed to offer the interest and enjoyment for which she hoped. So she changed course, and after several years of hard study qualified as an educational pyschologist. I too may have helped our children recognize that life is about the building of community, human and divine, when I moved out of fulltime church work to help train community and youth workers at Westhill College, Birmingham, as well as to serve the growing Christian community movement (of which more later).

At the same time Peter and Kirsten have given Sue and me the privilege of sharing their search for life. We have been fascinated and stimulated by Peter's restless energy, which has found a multitude of outlets from dismantling every article he can lay his hands on, to more recently wrestling with the problems posed by advanced computer programming. At seventeen he introduced us to the theory of relativity through an imaginative children's story he wrote as a school project. Since then his interest in physics and "expert systems" have been new worlds to which he has gently introduced us. We have also shared his enjoyment of mountains and walking.

Kirsten seems to have an inexhaustible capacity to make friends. On her bedroom wall for many years was a map of Britain covered with a host of flags indicating where her companions lived. Over the years our home has seen a steady stream of these friends coming and going. We have admired the way she has caught up with life after her slow and difficult start and, despite feeling she might never "make it", has tackled and achieved some demanding assignments – from passing her driving test to getting through university.

Peter and Kirsten have responded to the spiritual dimension of life in their own way and at their own pace – Peter more quietly, Kirsten more enthusiastically. But in both cases it has been a genuine and life-giving response which has deepened our own appreciation of the different ways in which God shares the journey with each of us.

Our family life has enabled all of us to share in the divine work of creation. We have discovered something of the meaning of liberation. We have gained insight into what the fellowship of the Holy Spirit is about. It has been an experience of community, as vivid as any time during our last major expedition as a foursome. We visited the States, travelling up and down the East Coast in an old minibus lent to us by some friends. Together we sampled the real America; from the Empire State Building in New York to the Smokey Mountains of North Carolina, from Southern Baptist fundamentalism to the Quakerism of Pendle Hill, from humming birds to rattlesnakes. Through the new horizons opened up, the friends we made and the sheer enjoyment we had, this trip epitomized for me what could come of saying "Yes" to life together.

Of course there have been many occasions when each of us has said "No" to life. Such times have been hard work because we have lost touch with one another for considerable stretches of the way. But we have kept going and joined up again. These difficult periods have done nothing to undermine my conviction that in our small unit of human existence we have been helped by the creative, liberating and unifying power of the Trinity to discover more about, and to help bring a little nearer, the coming of the kingdom community.

Yet important as they are, home and family are not enough. Schumacher did not argue that "small is beautiful" and leave it at that.[16] His contention was that the small could help provide the vital personal dimension needed to humanize our major institutions, not that the latter were redundant. George Simpson puts it another way:

> There has . . . been much discussion of the need for a return to primary (face-to-face) groups. But what is needed is a return to the ideals of the primary group in such a shape and so adjusted as to be capable of application to cosmopolitan conditions. Otherwise, a sort of return to the communal womb is being urged, a nostalgia for the infantile.[17]

Likewise the search for the kingdom community must be pursued beyond the small group of kin or intimate friends if our planet and world are to fulfil the divine purposes of the Trinity; if not only the life of the family but that of suburbs like Woodhouse, inner-city neighbourhoods like West Greenwich, cities like Birmingham or nations like Britain, are to be transformed. I now turn to that challenge, and the role of the church within it.

CHAPTER 3

Life Denied

1. Institutionalizing the Kingdom Community

The kingdom community is already here. We encounter its presence in the life-giving, liberating and unifying work of the Trinity. Yet it is a community in the process of being brought to fulfilment through a continuing exchange of life and love. The journey has begun but still lies before us.

For our generation, as with all others, that journey is about making the hope of glory a reality, about giving practical expression to our vision. This requires not only the proclamation of the message of life, freedom and unity, but earthing it in human affairs.

The journey has to be pursued in groups informal and formal, through associations and organizations, as well as within institutions – the home, the school, the hospital, the factory, the council chamber. All institutions are important, but none more so than that which should have the furthering of the kingdom community as its primary responsibility, the church.

Avery Dulles specifies five models of the church – being a mystical community, a sacrament, a herald, a servant, and an institution.[1] Throughout history, the life of the church has reflected these models. Yet there have been major problems. Dulles writes: "One of the five [models] . . . cannot properly be taken as primary – and that is the institutional model".[2] The danger which has always faced the church is that the institutional aspect of its existence becomes so dominating and demanding that it drains the life out of its other functions. As a consequence, the church begins to see itself as synonymous with, rather than the servant and herald of, the kingdom community.

A short time ago my students came for an evening meal. In their kindness they came bearing gifts, one of which was an arrangement of chrysanthemums. At first glance it looked attractive. But then I noticed that it was made of plastic and lacked the living texture, the delicate colours and the vitality of real flowers. It was an attempt to freeze and to fossilize what should have been growing and blooming in its own way and at its own pace. If the church as institution seeks to usurp the place of the kingdom community, it will not only freeze and fossilize the latter but be drained of life itself. It will distort the true nature of the kingdom, cutting itself off from the source of its own inspiration and renewal.

Unfortunately, there are today indications that this is just what is happening and, as a result, bringing the institutional church to the point of crisis. It is not simply a question of statistics, though my own Methodist Church has lost some 300,000 members since the early 'sixties. More important has been the ebbing away of vitality and energy from an institution which now appears to some observers to be increasingly like the dinosaur[3] at the end of its evolutionary era. Life is not being exchanged but denied. The kingdom community is not being furthered but neglected, and the journey towards it abandoned.

2. Life?

One of the most revealing features about any institution is its physical appearance. The buildings in which it operates tell us a great deal about the attitudes and concerns of the people it serves. This is especially true of the church, for Christians have gone out of their way to make the buildings in which they worship "symbolic places".[4] Church buildings fulfil far more than a purely functional purpose; they are, by chance or design, objects onto which men and women have projected a multitude of emotions, religious and otherwise. The consequences of this have often been as unfortunate as they have been beneficial.

The largest of my churches in Woodhouse was an ex-Wesleyan building opened amidst much local rejoicing in 1879. It was a tall square church of two storeys, constructed of heavy grey blocks of Yorkshire stone. It was a building of little beauty, the word "imposing" being the greatest compliment I could pay it. Around the church was a stone wall, except in front of the main entrance where there were tall railings and iron gates. Once through the gates one was faced by two solid wooden doors invariably closed except on Sundays. The building thus took on the appearance of a fortress, offering a formidable façade to any who might get too close. The message it communicated was "Keep out!"

It seemed to me that it was not just indigenous Woodhouse residents who were thus encouraged to pass by, but that God, the Creator of this living and lovely planet, was himself all but excluded. If one did approach intent on worship, the church and its grounds offered few signs of natural life – no shrubs or bushes, flowers or lawns – to lift one's spirits above the weight of stone and mortar. It was to me a place, like so many other churches of its kind, which did nothing to reveal the creative activity of God and the glory of the world he had brought into being.

If Woodhouse Wesley appeared to shut out God as well as the "irreligious" (an interesting combination), it also seemed to imprison the congregation. It was to the eternal credit of an omnipresent God and of those who attended services there that genuine worship did take place at all. But it was a struggle. Small windows meant that only a limited amount of light entered the sanctuary. Thus the interior of the building, especially gloomy when the sun failed to shine, and filled with row upon row of dark brown pews upstairs and down, was not exactly designed to lift one's heart in adoration and praise to the Lord of light and life.

The object that dominated the scene for most worshippers was the high central pulpit, large enough for the preacher to stroll round in comfort. The sanctuary was designed to ensure that his presence and his words, multitudes of them in most services, were the major focus of attention. If eyes did stray from this focal point, they would alight on the choir which sat immediately behind. One then had the choice of inspecting at leisure the attire of its members or, behind them, the large organ with its demonstrative array of pipes. One might also steal a glance at the brass vases on the communion table, the plaques on the wall or the piano at the side, all commemorating past benefactors.

I always felt that such visual aids pointed far more to the glory of man (and occasionally woman) than the glory of God the supreme benefactor. I felt them to be more often barriers than doors to an exchange of life with him. Thus the architecture, furnishings and ethos of the church seemed to lock us into, at best, a devout and sombre religious world or, at worst, a world that had never grasped the vibrance of the kingdom community and how to celebrate with zest and joy the life-giving gifts of the Creator.

No small price was exacted for the upkeep of this edifice. With a congregation slowly dwindling when I was there, and continuing to do so after I moved on, the financial burden was considerable. I learnt at Woodhouse both to admire and to despair of people's attitude to this aspect of Christian stewardship. I admired my members' readiness to give so much of their spare time and energy to renovate, paint and clean the church. I was impressed by their energetic commitment to raising much needed funds. At Wesley this was epitomized by the Christmas Market. Nearly every church organization worked long and hard for its "success", the latter being defined as a larger sum raised than in the year before. The day of the market itself, together with the build-up to it, far outweighed in effort and passion any other occasion in the church calendar.

That is why I also despaired. It seemed to me that Christian stewardship was being largely interpreted by my loyal Woodhouse church members as the preservation of a building, more a symbol of tribal identity and endeavour than of the limitless life and boundless love of God for all his creatures. So all-consuming could the former become that the needs of the wider world were largely screened out.

We did hold occasional bread and cheese lunches to raise money for the starving, but they were poorly attended. There were the usual "retiring collections" for the victims of natural disasters, or for the work of the National Children's Home. But for the congregation as a whole, charity usually began and ended at home. Even the situation of the crumbling and dishevelled village around us was no more than a passing topic of conversation for vague regret.

These aspects of church life in Woodhouse gave one little incentive, in Studdert-Kennedy's words, "to give and give, and give again, what God hath given thee"; at least in relation to other than the home team. Nor was there much of Teilhard's vision of the whole of life as one great sacrament in which we receive from all quarters God's gifts of grace, and in return offer ourselves and our possessions in the service of the kingdom community wherever that can be advanced.

As the Methodist minister in Woodhouse at that time, I bear as much responsibility as anyone else for this state of affairs. I was lacking in ability and courage to proclaim what I knew of the nature of God the Creator. I failed to bring a spirit of celebration into worship, and did little to challenge or redirect the time and energy spent on the upkeep of premises. The strength of the attitudes and practices of a congregation which, in relation to Christian stewardship at

least, seemed to direct the power of community inwards,
defeated me.

★   ★   ★   ★   ★

Is the story of one church typical of the way our buildings,
and much of what goes on within them, deny rather than
enhance life? It would be unfair to make sweeping
judgements. Yet on moving to West Greenwich in 1967, my
first commission was to shut a large Methodist church
which, only fifteen years before, had undergone major re-
pairs for bomb damage. This building was no more con-
ducive to celebrating life than any in Woodhouse; but here
people and money had actually run out.

There are of course many churches of breathtaking
loveliness and grandeur,[5] which unequivocally declare the
glory of God the Creator as well as celebrate the creativity of
man and woman. Most of our cathedrals point us majestically
in both directions. As late as the eighteenth century,
churches of great beauty and dignity were still being built to
enable people to "lift up their hearts" in adoration and praise.
But, as with Methodism, the nineteenth century took most
church architecture into a cul-de-sac.

Many of the neo-Gothic Anglican churches of that era
were a futile attempt to import a medieval past into a new
urban and industrial world. They were often grotesquely
large and culturally quite out of place. They appeared to be
more an attempt to ensure the existence of an acre or two of
holy ground in a foreign land than to witness to the life of
the city as the focus of God's creative activity. At best, they
were a place of refuge from a harsh world; at worst, they
became religious ghettos for the devout few. Those
buildings that do remain are as much alien to today's world
as any in Woodhouse. The kingdom community, as well as
the secular world, has moved on to a new stage of the
journey.

The problem is that such churches remain to distort our understanding of celebration and stewardship. They consume the devotion, time, effort and giving of those whose Christian calling should be leading them to put their energies into kingdom concerns. We have to find new places in which to worship, new ways of worshipping and new occasions on which to do it which will glorify God and not our forefathers or ourselves. We have to break free from an attitude to buildings and an understanding of "stewardship" which have more to do with a self-preservation society than a kingdom community seeking how to bring new life to a new age.

3. Liberation?

When I was in Woodhouse the notice board outside one of my churches displayed the words "Resident Minister" in bold lettering, with the address of the Methodist manse beneath; but never my actual name. It was to remind me that I was a bird of passage (no minister had ever stayed longer than six years), and that responsibility for the affairs and continuity of the life of the local church was in the hands of the pillars of the church in the local Leaders' Meeting. Conservative forces of this kind weakened my attempts to bring the message of Christ the Liberator to the people amongst whom I worked.

Any minister seeking to represent Christ is called to do his or her utmost to affirm each person as unique and of infinite value in the eyes of God. I soon encountered a number of constraints preventing me from fulfilling such a role. For example, I was expected to give virtually all my energies to the needs of my church members. Not only did they pay me (in Methodism, although the scale of stipends is decided by the Methodist Conference they are paid from local sources), but their pastoral demands were considerable. In a village like Woodhouse, I was regularly alerted to criticisms of having called on Mrs Jones but having missed out Mrs Brown, not because Mrs Brown was in particular need but because favours had to be distributed equally. I increasingly felt that I wanted to support certain members, not least in the younger age bracket, more fully than the time required to keep the remainder happy allowed.

This problem was made more acute by the fact that only one section of my members was readily accessible: mothers with young children, the retired and the sick. I had no objection to a ministry of pastoral care to these groups, but I felt that those struggling day by day to bear a Christian witness in the life of the secular city were often thereby devalued. As most evenings and weekends were packed tight with church meetings and events, these members hardly ever got a visit from me.

There was even less time left to make personal contact of any depth with non-churchgoers. I was involved in seeing people through the normal rites of birth, marriage and death. Some of these occasions, like comforting bereaved families after a pit disaster or the loss of a child in a road accident, were very important. But duty at the crematorium, where I was the foreman of a kind of production line in reverse, seemed to me a travesty of my role.

During my time in Sheffield and London, a few stalwarts from the local churches undertook visitations of the neighbourhoods. These at least enabled me to take "legitimate" time to meet non-churchgoers on a face-to-face basis and to show that we were concerned about them, whether or not they attended worship. But they were relatively short-lived projects, and the few of us engaged in this task must have appeared very much as ships passing in the night.

All this meant that my hopes of laying the foundations for a relationship which could lead men and women towards a liberating experience of Christ were severely circumscribed by the demands, some more legitimate than others, of certain sections of the "faithful". Yet even my ministry to the latter left me with major misgivings.

At the heart of the matter lay the fact that many of my members, adults in other respects, held Christian beliefs dominated by childhood experiences. Growing in the faith seemed to have petered out after their Sunday School days. By the 1960s even the teaching in the latter was coming apart at the seams. In Sheffield, the Sunday School remained Victorian in style, at one of my churches the children sitting restlessly in formal circles on wooden boxes in which they kept their hymn books and bibles. Lessons were well-intentioned but very traditional, with much reliance having to be placed on the willing rather than the properly trained helper. In West Greenwich we made something of a breakthrough in modern teaching methods. Yet we were still dogged, as in Sheffield, by lack of good staff. Even with the most imaginative of programmes it proved impossible to hold more than a handful of young people much after the age of thirteen.

Because of decades of neglect of any continuing form of adult Christian education, it was thus not surprising that the faith of many in Woodhouse and West Greenwich remained childish rather than childlike. My women's meetings, for example, still regarded texts picked out of a "blessing box" as an important form of spiritual nourishment. Yet ignorance of the Bible was also rife. One Sunday morning in Greenwich, the adults were covered with confusion by their lack of knowledge when the young people unexpectedly presented them with a questionnaire on simple biblical facts.

How then could one help people to realize their God-given potential when they had little knowledge or understanding of Christ's call to liberating service? How could one enable people to relate faith to life, when the only thing an elderly Woodhouse layman could suggest, when we encountered some minor misbehaviour amongst our young people, was that we pin up in every room a poster listing the ten commandments?

I myself did not help matters by falling victim to a pastoral role assumed to be one of offering reassurance and comfort, and not of challenging or raising difficult questions. Over ten years I gradually became adept at exchanging pleasantries and steering clear of confrontation. This meant that any hope of jolting my members into taking stock of their situation, let alone seeking a new beginning, was sacrificed on the altar of expediency. It was just too risky and disquieting for me to throw off the image of an all-caring father in God.

The official means of bringing people to a point of personal commitment to Christ was church membership. Each year a few of our young people and adults took preparation classes and went on to be confirmed. Yet many of them treated it as a formality, merely fulfilling the hopes of parents or spouses. They were lacking in enthusiasm and eagerness to discover more or go further. Neither heart nor head was really engaged.

In a vain attempt to explore the relevance of faith to work, I twice attempted to gather a group of members who were day school teachers, in order to raise pertinent educational issues. The gatherings were interesting but we found that, even when in a similar occupation, those living in the same neighbourhood did not necessarily have much in common. The local church did not seem to be the appropriate unit around which to base such an initiative.

There were of course more than a few of my members who by drawing on an array of resources – family, friends, conferences, travel, books – surmounted all these hurdles and found a liberating faith. In fact, I came to believe even more firmly in the grace of a living Christ because he seemed able to awaken, call and send people in search of fulfilment and wholeness when all the odds were against it.

But most of the churches I knew at first-hand during this time did little to enable their members to grow to true Christian maturity.

* * * * *

In 1973 I left Methodist circuit work to join the staff of Westhill College in Birmingham. What finally decided me to change direction was the fact that Methodism was unable to find a way of allowing me to work halftime at St Mark's, my church in West Greenwich, and halftime on the staff of Dartmouth House, a nearby lay training centre for the Anglican diocese of Southwark. This Centre was pioneering imaginative new approaches to adult education of which I very much wanted to be a part. But as ever, the demands of the pastoral ministry took precedence.

At a deeper level, however, my decision to move to what is known in Methodism as a ministry in "other appointments", was a growing conviction that I could no longer work with integrity in a situation where an understanding of personal salvation seemed so circumscribed. I had come to believe that the church, national and local, clerical and lay, was mistaking a staging post along the way for the destination. It appeared to me that the church, in its eagerness to ensure that man and woman were made and remained "religious", or even "Christian", was losing sight of the divine intent that we should grow towards wholeness first and foremost as human beings. We seemed more concerned to socialize people into an institution, be that national or local, than to prepare them for the life of the kingdom community. Our preoccupation was "church growth" (or church survival), not personal growth to enable men and women to be partners in the transformation of a secular world.

One consequence is that all denominations act most of the time as if entry into their fellowship assures salvation.

Nothing more needs be done. Here guidance in the spiritual life peters out (if it ever began), here instruction in the faith ceases, here Christian education ends, here major questions about belief are no longer on the agenda. The idea that liberation in Christ is meant to free us for a continuing journey of surprise, discovery and considerable personal change is quite foreign. The thought that we may along the way go through numerous cycles of doubt and bewilderment, as well as a spiritual re-awakening to new horizons, hardly comes into the reckoning. To encourage such a view of the journey towards salvation still borders on heresy. This is why many of my church members felt it was dangerous to read *Honest to God*[6] when it was published in 1963, and spoke disparagingly of the then Bishop of Woolwich. This is why, today, the Bishop of Durham is branded as unfit for episcopal office.

Because the church, national and local, takes socialization into its beliefs and practices as synonymous with entry into the kingdom community, obedience takes the place of liberation in Christ. The rules, formal and informal, are upheld and imposed by priest and laity alike, for both are predominantly concerned about the survival of the system.

In Methodism, it is usually loyalty to the local "cause", and a readiness to roll up one's sleeves and get involved, that are hallmarks of "true" membership. "I'm going to take my bed up there one day!" remarked a Woodhouse member to me with feeling. For more evangelical churches, and in the past for Methodism too, the criterion for entry may be conversion, backed up by "the gifts of the Spirit". Though Roman Catholics accept that baptism puts us all on the right road to the kingdom, regular attendance at mass is still regarded as the yardstick of full salvation by most of its members. Herein lies the "true" sign of belonging. For Anglicans, the entry requirements seem a bewildering mixture. They encompass aspects of those associated with every other denomination, accompanied by a hidden assumption that many confirmation candidates wish to be members of a nationally approved ecclesiastical body.

Just as each church lays down its particular regulations for personal salvation, so too does it emphasize certain cultural and ethical requirements. For me as a lad, giving public expression to my Methodist label was virtually equivalent to not drinking, not gambling and not purchasing goods from shops on Sundays. I was well into my 'twenties, and had been a keen rugby player for years, before I allowed alcohol to pass my lips. Even now I still feel a slight pang of guilt when entering a pub. Every church, however, is engaged in raising its would-be members' awareness to these hallmarks, formal and informal, of salvation. Whether they relate to the issue of birth-control, to the use of alcohol, to the status of women or to appropriate attire for worship, these signs of belonging remain central to what each denomination sees as being a "Christian".

Such powerful forces of socialization take time and energy to maintain. This is why so much effort still goes into training clergy as shepherds of the flock, and why the faithful lay person assumes the former's task to be essentially that of maintaining the institution, local or national. The priest or minister is there, first, to preserve the traditions of the past and, secondly, to socialize newcomers into it. He is often as much a symbolic figure of a closed ecclesiastical system as is the symbolic place in which he leads worship. If he does venture out to engage with a secular world he often takes with him the image of a select and rather remote religious club, not of a lively and eager travelling company in search of the kingdom community.

The different meanings which churches give to personal salvation are not the result of any consciously dishonest intent. They are a consequence of a long history during which the part has time and again been mistaken for the whole, the port of call for the destination. But the situation is now reaching crisis point for two main reasons. One is that the differing views of salvation offered now cancel each other out. A feature of a pluralistic, not to mention secular, society is that all values become relative. The other is that many people simply do not find the brands of salvation on offer liberating. They appear restrictive and inward-looking, more the acceptance of dead "truths" than a journey towards abundant life. Indeed, what is available within the secular world often appears to give a greater sense of dynamic, and even divine, purpose and personal fulfilment.

In 1985 I wrote an article in the "Face to Faith" column of *The Guardian*.[7] In it I described what the churches define as the essential marks of salvation as, at best, lay-bys along the route. I received over sixty letters in reply, nearly all of which came from people longing to be off on the next stage of the journey yet feeling lonely and unsupported. Many saw norms of church allegiance as a dead weight holding them back. The options seemed to be to accept captivity with resignation or to break clear into the unknown, with a sense of anticipation and yet with apprehension and guilt. Unless we who claim to be the church gain a new and life-giving vision of what it means to be liberated by Christ, to be whole persons, it will be we who remain captive, and those who journey on who find true salvation.

4. Unity?

"The old is passing away; the new is incapable of being born." These were words spoken by Bill Gowland to a course I attended some years ago at the Luton Industrial Mission. Nothing could be more true of the church's attempt to bear witness to the unity of the Holy Spirit.

In Woodhouse, those who regularly attended worship

and church meetings had a strong sense of belonging. My two main churches contained many members related by kinship ties, at Wesley with a family of six brothers and sisters and their relations filling many offices. Two of this family were referred to as "Uncle" and "Auntie" even by those unrelated to them. Most prominent members of my church had resided in the village for the whole of their lives, for some of them the church virtually becoming a second home. Around it revolved most of their leisure activities and to it, as we have seen, they committed a significant percentage of their worldly wealth.

Yet though this situation gave the members of my Woodhouse churches a powerful sense of solidarity, it also created problems. Those moving into the area were not only unattracted by the buildings and traditional forms of worship, but had little hope of gaining more than superficial acceptance within such a close-knit group. They were "incomers", politely welcomed if they appeared, but given responsibility with reluctance. At the same time, however, the old families were steadily fragmenting, broken up by death, or by their younger members moving away to be educated, obtain work or to live in more salubrious neighbourhoods. The old church was passing away, and has continued to do so since I left, but the new church seemed incapable of being born.

To move to West Greenwich was to step into a very different world. The United Presbyterian and Methodist congregation at St Mark's contained only a few families related by birth or marriage, and even fewer who had resided in the area all their lives. Most members had opted to join, rather than been brought up in, that church. They were widely dispersed over south-east London, travelling in on Sunday mornings to worship. Immediately afterwards they "scattered like rats leaving a sinking ship", as one of my church leaders vividly described it. Few attended weeknight meetings, though special social events on Saturday evenings were reasonably popular.

If Woodhouse was dominated by the "locals",[8] West

75

Greenwich was in the hands of the "cosmopolitans". The latter enjoyed an easy-going and open type of Christian fellowship, which enabled newcomers to find a niche quickly and to move on without fuss if they so desired. Yet here, too, there were difficulties.

The main problem was the unwillingness of most members of St Mark's to give a great deal of time to the work of the church over and above Sunday worship and the occasional weeknight event. Hence the Sunday School suffered, and keeping the church well maintained was a constant anxiety. Here was an open fellowship but, apart from a small core of members, one with nowhere near as strong a sense of solidarity as I had found in Woodhouse.

West Greenwich brought home to me that a church which comes to rely on Sunday worship alone as the mainstay of fellowship will find the bonds between Christian people steadily getting weaker.[9] Worship by itself has never been sufficient to maintain a dynamic sense of unity. In the past, the rural parish church, the churchyard, and sometimes the church itself, were the scenes of frequent social events from markets to merrymaking. In Woodhouse in the 'sixties the formality and solemnity of worship were offset by many lively social gatherings. We cannot return to the experience of the village. But for Christians to try to make do with the superficiality of a brief Sunday encounter is to deny the fellowship of the Spirit and thus of the kingdom community.

We thus seem caught between two stools. My Woodhouse churches possessed a strong but narrow sense of solidarity; in West Greenwich the church was more open to newcomers, but the sense of belonging was a good deal weaker. The old church is dying, but the new is not yet born.

This situation is not helped by the continuing captivity of Christians to denominational allegiances.[10] In Woodhouse my two churches originally belonged to different branches (mini-denominations) of Methodism. The Wesleyan church was opened in 1879. Ten years later St Paul's, a United Methodist Free Church, was built two hundred yards from Wesley. In 1905, a Primitive Methodist chapel was also built between the two, though this had to close in 1951. At national level all these branches of Methodism had merged by 1932. Yet thirty years later Woodhouse Wesley and St Paul's remained separate and independent. I myself, as well as my predecessors and successors, spent innumerable hours and much effort seeking to bring the two slowly ageing congregations together – but to no avail.

This situation had certain positive aspects. No two churches could have survived as long if they had not possessed members so loyal and dedicated to their survival, and so tenacious in fending off all external threats. For this one could not help but admire them. But I believe the negative consequences to be more telling. One problem was the friction and even hostility which rivalry between the two congregations sometimes caused. A few years after I left, a major division occurred between those opting for one united church and those against, which led to defections and bitterness. Another problem was the waste of money, time and energy (not least of the minister) needed to maintain two congregations which duplicated the whole gamut of Sunday and weekday activities.

If the Methodists of Woodhouse had problems over local unity, the church nationally was not doing much better. A year after I arrived in Sheffield, the "Conversations" between the Anglican and Methodist Churches in England got underway. For the remainder of my time there, as well as for my first two years in London, I was engaged in many hours of endeavour to enable my members to understand and debate the issues involved. They never really understood them, in the end voting in favour of the national unity scheme but also voting against Methodist bishops (a proviso on which the scheme was founded!) The Methodist Conference approved the scheme in 1969, only to find the Anglican Convocations had rejected it. Three years later the same story was repeated. A decade later, even an attempt to "covenant" together met a similar fate.

My experience of other initiatives in Christian unity at this time did not offer any more hope of a lasting breakthrough. In West Greenwich, the Spirit triumphed over apprehension and stubbornness to enable our first united Presbyterian Methodist church to be established. (The Presbyterians subsequently have joined nationally with the Congregationalists, and are known as the United Reform Church.) Though a handful of members left in protest, the congregations, small as they were, had taken a bold and positive step of faith. Yet almost immediately after the joint venture had been inaugurated, the Methodist Conference sought to move me to another appointment, thus threatening to undermine in its infancy the team ministry and the united church on which it had been built. Although this proposal was withdrawn, the Methodist appointment has since been terminated and the joint congregations are now served by the United Reform minister alone.

During my six years in West Greenwich, my Presbyterian colleague and I were members of a lively ecumenical group of ministers and clergy, including an outstanding Roman Catholic priest. When he departed, and despite ardent pleas to his bishop for a suitable replacement, he was followed by a priest totally apathetic about things ecumenical. The failure of the Anglicans to appoint a suitable successor to their parish priest when he had to retire through illness, meant the final curtain for what might eventually have led to a breakthrough for the churches in West Greenwich in their pursuit of a wider understanding and expression of Christian unity.

* * * * *

If my move out of Methodist circuit work in 1973 was in part the result of my inabilty to live with the institutional church's view of personal salvation, it was given further impetus by my unwillingness to accept its understanding of corporate salvation.

I had been brought up through home, local church, national service and university, to know how life-enriching Christian fellowship could be. What I had been privileged to experience as the unifying power of the Spirit had both depth and breadth. Yet this I could neither find, nor myself succeed in fostering in any lasting way over the first ten years of my ministry.

In Sheffield I found churches wherein there was a deep sense of belonging, but one which was socially and spiritually narrow and hindered rather than encouraged an open fellowship. In West Greenwich I enjoyed the easy- going and flexible nature of the church's life, but apart from the faithful few there seemed little desire to deepen relationships beyond a brief encounter on Sunday mornings. Neither of these situations fitted my understanding of what the kingdom community should be about.

On the national church scene I experienced even more disappointment. At theological college, and for ten years after that, I had been presented with exhortation after exhortation to promote Christian unity between the different denominations, and had risen with enthusiasm to the challenge. I had been an avid student of the doctrinal debate that surrounded the Anglican-Methodist "Conversations", and had done my utmost to present the issues clearly and fairly to my church members. Spurred on by radical developments in other churches, not least the Second Vatican Council, my hopes for the unity of the Christian Church in the United Kingdom in the relatively near future were high. Thus the rejection of Methodism by the Church of England was a body blow.

For the next few years my energies went into trying to

make Christian unity work at the local level. The emergence of St Mark's as a united church, and the work of the West Greenwich ecumenical team, were exciting endeavours. But the failure of the British churches to draw together nationally (the emergence of the United Reform Church in 1972 was hardly a breakthrough), meant that progress towards genuinely new and sustainable forms of unity on the local scene were hindered at every step. St Mark's is still there and exercising a valuable ministry to the neighbourhood, but the Methodist contribution is becoming increasingly attenuated. Other ecumenical ventures across West Greenwich as a whole have come and gone at the whim of passing clergy.

The fact is, I believe, that the church local and national has not yet glimpsed what corporate salvation for our day and age must mean. It has seen neither the glory nor understood the cost of Christian unity. Its head knows what the New Testament says about Christians being one in the Spirit, and it sings with gusto about "one church, one faith, one Lord", but it lacks the vision, the will and the skill to turn such sentiments into reality. So the belief that unity amongst Christians is vital and urgent for the advancement of the kingdom community dies a natural death, suffocated by the church's refusal to exchange life in any meaningful way. It is enough for salvation to be faithful Methodists, Anglicans, Roman Catholics or whatever, even if "the twain" rarely meet. This is a disastrous situation.

It is a disaster for the church on the purely practical level. If there is "one faith" and "one Lord", then it is a denial of Christian stewardship to keep so many redundant buildings and to waste the money, time and energy of the people of God in trying to maintain them. If only to conserve resources, the rationalization of plant, property and personnel is now an urgent necessity. There is no shortage of places of worship and of clergy to staff them; it is simply that we insist on running parallel shows, each of which requires a full cast of performers and stagehands.

More important, the drain on resources resulting from this situation means that finance and personnel are not available to support the furthering of the kingdom community where the going is rough and the needs of the world acute. My own church cannot support many ministries unrelated to established circuit work because of a "shortage" of money and ministers. If the Anglican-Methodist "Conversations" had been successful, more resources urgently needed for missionary initiatives might have become available. The reality is, however, that all denominations remain the prisoners of "surburban captivity", and their ability to engage in more than the survival of a narrow form of ecclesiastical system is undermined.

Yet the failure of the church to grasp the nettle of Christian unity has more profound repercussions than the issue of wasted resources. If the church behaves as just one more human tribe, alongside all the rest, self-centred, possessive and fragmented, it can have little more than good advice to offer to those struggling to find the root causes of human division, conflict and violence. If the church simply reflects the disunity of secular society, and in such places as South Africa and Northern Ireland openly promotes division, what earthly use is it to those striving to create one world?

No church which condones its own schisms and fails to use all its skills, theological and sociological, to help address the deep causes of human disunity, can hope to be a sign of the kingdom community in our day and age. No such church has anything of substance to offer to those addressing themselves to such issues as gender, race and class, let alone peace and justice. If the physician does not know how to heal himself, how can he heal others?

5. The Search Continued

My move to Birmingham in 1973 was away from a church which for me felt as though it were denying life, not least life together. It was an attempt to break free of a ministry constricted by the upkeep of symbolic places, many of which were signs of the end, not the beginning of an era.

It was a move to be free of a profession which put making men and women religious before enabling them to become fully human. I believed that God was calling us to explore a vast and rich diversity of ministries on behalf of the kingdom community, of which the institutional church knew how to affirm and nurture only a tiny proportion. The world teemed with opportunities. Yet we were hemmed in by an ecclesiastical conception of vocation from beginning to end. I yearned to be able to define "Christian" in more life-giving and liberating terms than the role of a parochial and pastoral ministry allowed.

My change of occupation was an attempt to break clear of the church's limited understanding of Christian fellowship, be it of a local or a cosmopolitan kind. It was, too, an endeavour to end the claustrophobia of being tied to the values, norms and practices of one denomination, however well that had nurtured and guided me in the past.

I did not see my move into secular employment as a rejection of the church, or of my call to be an ordained minister within it – in fact, the very reverse. It was because, through the witness of some fine Christian people in Sheffield, London and well beyond, I had been given a vision of the kingdom community and the church's vital role as its servant and herald, that I felt compelled to go in search of a new way forward. It was because I was convinced that the survival of human community was intimately bound up with the coming of the kingdom community, and that it was the church's task to bear witness to that truth, that I could not remain for the rest of my ministry within the traditional fold. So I changed direction, not simply to find another kind of job which could support me on the journey, though that was essential, but to go in search of the signs of the kingdom community.

At the same time the search for my own soul and my own salvation continued. It was not only as a minister of religion that I felt the need of liberation and new life, but as a human being. Many influences, domestic, economic, educational and political, were opening up fresh vistas; and I had to do more than acknowledge these from afar. Life had to be lived, not only reflected on, and that meant having "the courage to be" and to do, not just to stand on the edge of things and dip in my toe.

This change of direction was also an attempt to re-discover the life and energy at the heart of the kingdom community. I went in search of a God who was not only Creator, Liberator and Unifier, but all three in One. I was looking for a God who was showing me that the purpose of living was the perfection of all things, not in the form of some static ecclesiastical institution but in a never ceasing life-giving exchange of love. I wanted to be part of this quest for life, even if it took me, as Tillich once put it, into a land "without a name, a church, a cult, a theology".[11] I was determined to get out of what had become my lay-by and press on with my journey.

CHAPTER 4

Life Discovered

1. On the Margins and in the Cracks

On 2nd August 1970 I was present at a very unusual gathering. It was billed as a "Festival of Communes". A thousand or more people, most in their twenties, some with young children in tow, converged on the Roundhouse, in Chalk Farm, London. They were attired in the garb of the day: the women in maxi-length dresses, second-hand clothes and bare feet; the men in Levi jeans and sandals, with long hair and beards. It was a "happening", with people milling gently around in an apparently aimless way, smoking the odd "joint", or listening to the group on the stage playing an assortment of bongo drums, tambourines, beer cans and sticks.

I had gone to the festival purely out of curiosity. London was at this time the epicentre of the so-called "counter-culture" which had been given impetus during the preceding years by the Beatles, by a "Youthquake",[1] by protest movements in the United States focused first on civil rights and then on the war in Vietnam, by student riots in France and elsewhere in 1968, and by the emergence of the "permissive society".

One particular consequence of these years of social and political ferment was the emergence of the commune. Its rise to prominence was remarkable. At the end of 1969, the *Communes Journal* had a circulation of seven hundred; by the middle of 1970 it had risen to two thousand five hundred. The Festival of Communes at the Roundhouse typified the rapid growth in the number of young people who were prepared to break with the traditions of the 'fifties and early 'sixties to pursue an alternative lifestyle, anywhere from Eel Pie Island on the Thames at Twickenham, to Findhorn in the north-east of Scotland, from the heart of Notting Hill to a remote Welsh hill farm near Barmouth.

As the minister of a relatively straight middle class congregation in West Greenwich, my first-hand experience of such groups was, to say the least, limited. In 1969, a priest friend of mine, together with a few other friends, had set up what they called the Blackheath Commune just down the road from our manse. Another ministerial colleague had, about this time, taken himself off to give holy communion to some members of a large commune which had set up shop in Piccadilly. So to get more of the feel of this burgeoning movement I donned my counter-culture gear and spent the day at the Roundhouse, coming away bemused but fascinated.

I was fascinated because what was happening struck a chord. Whatever else it was or was not, the commune movement seemed to be about a search for life, over against the dead hand of institutions. To many it would seem more than a little weird to dance half-naked in the moonlight on the hills of Wales, or to talk to cabbages to help them grow bigger at Findhorn! But despite the more eccentric face of the commune movement, those involved were vitally and vibrantly alive.

The communards were seeking an intimate relationship with the world of nature and revelled in its beauty and vitality. They were in search of a sense of personal freedom. They wanted to be themselves, and to be themselves fully. "Doing one's own thing" or, more idealistically, "self-actualization" were the "in" phrases. For some, this might be little more than an ego-trip. But for others, going to live communally meant the opportunity to learn and use new skills, to discover more about oneself through close contact with others, and to shape one's own destiny.[2]

I was also fascinated because the commune movement was about "getting it together", about a sense of belonging, about solidarity. At the Roundhouse, people simply shared – their food, drink, "joints", conversation, music. It was a gathering of "beautiful people", utopian in the extreme, but none the worse for that if it were a vision of a new heaven and a new earth you were after. And I was in search of such a vision, wherever the inspiration might come from.

A few weeks after the Roundhouse Festival I paid my first visit to the Island of Iona, having been invited to lead a week's conference at the abbey there. I knew vaguely of George MacLeod and his pioneering ministry in Glasgow, and a little about the Iona Community itself, mainly because our church at St Mark's was Presbyterian with many Scottish ties. But the experience of staying on the Island and meeting community members was a revelation. What I had learnt from the secular commune movement and my discoveries on Iona came together. For the first time I began to believe that the regeneration of the life of society and church might come from the margins or within the cracks. It was a glimmer of light on the horizon, but was it the first sign of a new dawn?

Eight years before I had experienced a similar sense of hope and excitement when I had arrived at a still relatively unknown village in central France. I was en route to Geneva, but had stopped off at Taizé out of interest to see the community of brothers who had been living and working there for some years. The two events of that short visit which I recall most vividly were arriving exhausted and at once graciously being offered food and a bed, and worship in the beautiful little village church accompanied by marvellous chanting of the psalms. For all its simplicity, Taizé was even then an intense experience of something new and vibrant coming to birth. It was akin to that which my passing acquaintance with the commune movement and then my visit to Iona brought to the fore.

I returned from Iona more certain than ever before that if the church were to break free from its institutional captivity, locally or nationally, then some powerful catalyst would be needed to make it aware of its parlous situation and rouse it to action. But could not such a catalyst be found within the structures as I knew them?

At this time, my last hope of finding a disturber within the fold lay with a body called "One for Christian Renewal". Since my days in Sheffield I had been a keen member of the Methodist Renewal Group, an association made up mainly of Methodist ministers who from the early 'sixties had been pressing for the radical transformation of the life of the church, not least in relation to Christian unity. The name of its magazine *New Directions* typified its concerns. In 1968, the Methodist Renewal Group took the lead in suggesting a new organization which would incorporate all the denominational "renewal groups" then in existence. The challenge was taken up, and in 1970 One for Christian Renewal came into being, bringing together radical young ministers and laity from all churches. The Catholic Renewal Group felt it politically inadvisable to join, but strongly backed the new initiative.

I served for many years on the Council both of the Methodist Renewal Group and of One for Christian Renewal. But though the latter was able to provide a useful support group, especially for frustrated young ministers, it never became the dynamic catalyst for which some of us ardently hoped. Because it was conceived within the institutional womb, it depended on the institution for much of its energy and could not easily develop a new model of the church. It was not long, therefore, before denominational renewal groups with fresh titles, such as the Alliance of Radical Methodists, began to appear once more.

So for me it was back to the Taizés and Ionas of this world. None the less, One for Christian Renewal did help my search in one major way. In 1971 its council readily backed my proposals to produce a broadsheet containing stories about Christians (and sometimes others) engaged in community building. Thus in the autumn of that year the first issue of the magazine *Community*, sixteen pages in all, was published. My first editorial began with these words:

> The institutional church is at a critical point in its history – and perhaps one of the overriding crises is the breakdown of old patterns of Christian community. Christian people in many places are frustrated and bewildered by the inability of the church to inspire even as much vitality and create even as dynamic a sense of community as the secular world. The old is dying and seems unable or unwilling to give birth to the new.[3]

Community has never had a circulation of more than seven hundred and fifty but it has now survived for a decade and a half, three times a year carrying self-portraits of their life and work written by Christian groups. Up to the present time about a hundred and fifty of them have been published.

When in 1973 I moved onto the staff of Westhill College, Birmingham, it opened up a wealth of opportunities to continue my search. One of these was time to travel. Because of my conviction that the catalyst for the regeneration of the church was the small (and, from my point of view, as yet undiscovered) Christian cell, and because I wanted good material for the *Community* magazine, I decided to use my vacations to get around and see for myself what, if anything, was really going on.

For the next three or four years I traversed the United Kingdom, often with my long-suffering family in tow, to visit groups of every shape, size and kind, from the south-west of England to the north of Scotland, from South Wales to Northern Ireland. In 1976, I crossed the Atlantic to explore whether anything similar was happening on both the East and West Coasts of the United States.

There is no space here to describe these often enthralling

journeys. For more information I can only refer the reader to a major book I wrote about my experiences in 1977,[4] to an overview of more recent developments, written in 1984,[5] and best of all to the back copies of *Community*.

As I visited the astonishing variety of groups which proved to be in existence, a number of their characteristics matched my growing understanding of the nature of the kingdom community. In the first place, they gained their vitality and energy from being "earthed", near to the ground, sometimes literally as well as metaphorically. They were groups existing at the "grassroots", finding that situation to be a source of new life, physically as well as spritually. They were living cells with a powerful potential for explosive growth and great creativity. This I saw as springing from their being closely in touch with a life-giving God and Creator.

In the second place, each group was unique and its members involved in their own particular search for freedom and fulfilment. Their callings and their ministries were thoroughly diverse and distinct. My first contacts had been with those, non-Christian and Christian, wanting to live together under one roof. But as I travelled the country, I also came across scores of non-residential groups searching out and attempting to build the kingdom community through their work, their service to those in need or through the pursuit of key issues of the day. This gave their journey a clear purpose and direction. To undertake this calling they met regularly to talk and plan and pray, but did not live together. I came to believe that these "apostolic" groups were just as significant for furthering the coming of the kingdom as those which had chosen to live communally. I sensed that these vocational groups in particular were drawing a great deal of their inspiration and energy from Christ the Liberator.

The third feature of the groups I encountered, residential and non-residential, was the strong sense of belonging which their members possessed. Most were face-to-face groups existing on a genuinely human scale and, even when apart, their members were in close and regular contact with one another. This often gave them a passionate feeling of solidarity. I felt that the source of this strong and intimate fellowship was very much the work of the Holy Spirit the Unifier.

These three features of the groups I visited were not as distinct as I have indicated here. To a degree, each group possessed them all. But some appeared to manifest one characteristic rather more strongly than the other two. At the same time, there was amongst many of them a growing awareness that, despite their uniqueness, they were engaged in a common search for life, liberation and unity, and the wholeness which that could bring. Though still more hidden than manifest, I believed there could here be emerging a new kingdom community movement in this country.

That this might be the case was by no means out of the question. The church traced its origins to a tribe wandering in the wilderness of Sinai, and to twelve men and their leader travelling the highways and byways of Palestine. It owed its continuing renewal to groups of monks, to bands of friars, to small congregations seeking its "re-formation", to "class meetings" generating a new enthusiasm for the faith, and to small companies of missionary adventurers. It was for me at this time an open but important question as to whether the groups I encountered were part of this prophetic Christian heritage.

What follows in the next three sections of this chapter can only be a glimpse of what inspired me on my travels, mainly during the 'seventies but sometimes in more recent years. Though a number of the groups have now disbanded, this does not matter. Others have taken their place. What does matter is the vision of the kingdom community to which they were bearing witness, and the way they were seeking, on the margins or within the cracks, to live out that vision amidst the often hard realities of the present age.

2. Life

It was a hair-raising ride! We were driven by the wife of one of the wealthiest landowners in Scotland at speeds reaching eighty miles an hour, from Inverness to the shores of Little Loch Broom in Wester Ross. It was planned as a flying visit to meet a number of her friends who had taken over a deserted crofting community at Scoraig in order to pursue a simple lifestyle based on a conservationist philosophy.

Three things impressed me about Scoraig during our very brief stay. First, the sheer beauty of the place. It could be bleak and cold in winter, or plagued with midges in high summer, but these hazards were more than offset by the quiet loveliness of Little Loch Broom and the majesty of An Teallach standing guard at its head. Then there was the sense of being deeply in touch with life and living. "It's a natural heaven for young children", said one of the mothers, "and no one has to organize playgroups with sand and water! There are animals about all the time; birth, mating and death are part of everyday life." Finally, there was the community itself; at that time two dozen adults who had had enough of the capitalist rat-race and wanted to live and work at the speed of the days and the seasons, bringing their families up in a way which would honour the planet and preserve its life-giving properties.

Tom, one of the community, had for some years worked in New York but had had enough of the noise, dirt and violence. As a member of the Iona Community, he had kept in close touch with the Western Highlands. So here he was in his mid-forties, seeking a new life in a new environment. Scoraig and Tom symbolized for me the longing of many people to re-establish a living relationship with the physical world, and with God its Creator and Preserver. Nor was it merely a coincidence that Tom had arrived there because of his links with Iona. That place too reminds one of the mystery and majesty of the created universe.

Kenneth Clark in his book *Civilization* writes of that tiny island in these words:

> I never come to Iona – and I used to come here almost every year when I was young – without feeling that "some God is in this place". It isn't as awe-inspiring as some other holy places – Delphi or Assisi. But Iona gives one more than anywhere else I know a sense of peace and inner freedom. What does it? The light, which floods round on every side? The lie of the land which, coming after the solemn hills of Mull, seems strangely like Greece, like Delos, even? The combination of wine-dark sea, white sand, and pink granite? Or is it the memory of those holy men who for two centuries kept western civilization alive?[6]

Like Kenneth Clark, what enthralled me on my first visit to Iona was the certainty that "some God is in this place"; not cooped up in a holy building, but exhilaratingly alive in the pounding seas, the white sands, the brilliant green of the grassy machair and the dark mountains of Mull. In this setting the abbey does not contain God, but simply focuses his presence like a magnifying glass held to catch the rays of the sun. Thus for the community and its many visitors the whole of Iona becomes a truly symbolic place, bringing men and women to a vivid awareness of the omnipresence of God the Creator.

Not many miles from Iona across the Irish Sea, another Christian community also takes a good deal of its inspiration from the glory of its surroundings. Nestling precariously on the cliffs of the North Antrim Coast is the country home of the Corrymeela Community, established in 1965 to promote reconciliation in that troubled Province. Their conference centre near Ballycastle is situated amidst the beautiful panorama of Rathlin Island, the North Channel, and Fair Head. "Corrymeela" is the Gaelic word for "the hill of harmony", and its location bears witness to that designation.

Many more Christian groups have "beaten a retreat" to the far corners of the earth, and back to the land. In South Wales, for example, several such groups cluster together under the shadow of the Black Mountains: Trefeca, the main conference centre of the Presbyterian Church of Wales; The Skreen, which offers a lovely setting for exploring Christian life and ministry in the context of a renewed spirituality: the small community of the Sisters of the Sacred Heart at Llanerchwen; and (in the planning stage) a l'Arche house for the mentally handicapped in Brecon.

But for many of these groups, omnipresence is not simply a matter of rediscovering God in the natural world and its rhythms. It is finding him everywhere.

En route to Iona in 1976, our family stayed at the Iona Community House in the centre of Glasgow (its work has now been transferred to other parts of the city). It was set up as a witness to a God present not only in the beauty of the Western Isles but in the heart of the secular city. Over forty groups made use of its facilities, from Alcoholics Anonymous to Women in Action, from the Simon Community to a group for agoraphobics. It was as dirty and ugly as Iona was clean and lovely. But both places were seen by the community as of equal importance.

In recent years the Iona Community has been establishing so-called Columban Houses (or flats) in cities across the country. Some twenty of these now exist, with three to six occupants in each, many of them unemployed young Christians. They are involved in helping with health centres, youth organizations, lunch clubs for the elderly, and discussion groups for those on the fringes of the church. "Col-

onies of heaven is what the Saint would have called them",
writes John Bell.[7]

So it is with Corrymeela. The spaciousness and loveliness
of Ballycastle are not used as a means of escape from the
realities of Belfast or Derry. They are meant to help people
find God, so that he can be recognized in the midst of
violence and suffering. Furthermore, the Corrymeela Community has a physical presence not only on the coast of
North Antrim, but in the homes of both Protestants and
Catholics, sometimes meeting apart, sometimes together, in
the cities and towns of Northern Ireland.

One of the outstanding memories of my visit to Northern
Ireland in the mid 'seventies was a week spent in a small
household of Anglican Franciscan friars just off the Shankill
Road, Belfast. We were situated only a little way from the
"peace line" which separated the Protestant and Roman
Catholic communities, and which then attracted a good deal
of violent attention. I recall during prayers one evening how
the reading of the psalms suddenly brought home to me
what it meant to feel deep anger and fear (and no doubt for
many in Belfast, hatred) in the presence of God. Yet this
was real worship, not in a church but in a small terraced
house on the edge of no-man's-land.

To be able to practise the presence of God unfettered by
the restrictions of religious buildings or religious rituals
opens up enormous possibilities. The creative and
sustaining power of God can then be focused, celebrated
and tapped into wherever we are and whenever we need it.
This frees men and women to worship God in fresh and
life-giving ways and with the whole of their experience.

The Iona Community has also grasped this nettle. One of
the happenings of any summer week on the island is not
only the worship in the abbey, with its emphasis on
celebration, peacemaking and healing, but the pilgrimage.
One walks to places of significance in the Christian history
of the island, not least the bay where St Columba landed

from Ireland in 563 A.D. At each port of call a brief act of worship is held, with the sea and the sky, the rocks and the sand, as an awe-inspiring backcloth.

On one of our visits, two pilgrimages met up, the normal Iona walk-about and the Pilgrims of St Francis, who had travelled from the mainland across Mull en route to Iona. The latter is a European group, set up between the wars in order to work for reconciliation, peace and justice. One form in which this is given expression is through their annual pilgrimage, during which participants converse together, share meals and worship as a group. "Our communion table is a pile of rucksacks, our bread is the left-over sandwiches, and our wine is a mug of tea", said one of them.

For a decade and more, one group which brought a new dimension to praise and prayer was the Community of Celebration, originating in Texas and coming to England in 1972. They drew inspiration from the early charismatic movement, and employed a wide variety of approaches to worship. When the Community of Celebration was at Yeldall Manor in Berkshire, I shared their open-air evening worship, which was a joyful combination of music, song and dance. From this community have come The Fisherfolk, a music and singing group which has made an outstanding contribution to worship across the United Kingdom and beyond. Its sister community, at Post Green in Dorset, developed "festive occasions" as a major part of its life, with celebrations taking place throughout the year – at a summer fête, a mid-winter festival, family "highdays" and community holidays.

Christian groups of this kind can of course also engage in the joyous celebration of the gifts of God the life-giver within buildings – even if sometimes with a difference. I enjoyed worship at St Julian's, the women's community near Horsham, because the east end of their chapel is constructed entirely of glass so that you can see the spacious garden beyond. One Whitsuntide at Ammerdown, near

Bath, I took part in a celebration which not only used words and music in imaginative ways, but took us in procession through many rooms of the house, so that the whole place could contribute to our worship.

As with the Franciscans in Belfast, many new Christian groups use the home as a focal point for thanksgiving and worship. Next to the open air, this for me is often the most real of worshipping environments, for it embraces within any act of celebration the ordinary things of everyday life. I have shared many moments – deeply aware of the presence of God – around kitchen tables, over meals or in living rooms, sometimes in the form of a eucharist or agape with homemade bread and wine, or water.

For Christian groups to leap from the small to the large assembly still remains possible, however. On a July Saturday in 1982, a thousand or more people came together in Wells Cathedral, not only to commemorate the eighth centenary of the birth of St Francis, but for "Celebrating Community". As well as exhibitions and workshops on "Painting Community", "Dancing Community", "Acting Community", "Unemployed Community" and "Disabled Community", there was a colourful and joyful final service which included all these aspects of life in a great act of praise and prayer.

This in-touchness with the physical world and God the Creator, and this ability to express his life-giving nature in worship in any location, carries over for many Christian groups into a strong desire to share in God's acts of creation and to strive to preserve this planet. Freed from the constraints of the upkeep of half-empty churches and expensive ecclesiastical buildings, they have skills and energy available for a creative and outgoing form of Christian stewardship.

We have in our living room a large array of attractive artefacts made by a variety of Christian groups. There is a brown earthenware pot made at Pilsdon in Dorset, bowls from Taizé, mugs from Taena in Gloucestershire, a children's jigsaw from Keveral Farm in Cornwall, and a coloured glass butterfly from a craft workshop in Glastonbury, to name but a few. They represent the desire felt by many Christians to use their skills of eye and hand to re-create things of beauty in partnership with God.

Some of the groups I have visited over the years take their understanding of stewardship further than this, dedicating their lives to farming or to smallholdings, wherever possible basing their methods on organic principles. These endeavours range from very modest projects, where little more than a back garden is involved, through places like Scoraig, to those using sophisticated technical skills and modern equipment, like Commonwork, a dairy farm in Kent. Nor is it only in rural areas that such ventures exist. In the heart of Sparkbrook, Birmingham, a Christian group called Ashram Acres Unlimited forms the core of a land-use project, reclaiming urban wasteland such as demolition sites and gardens which have become dumps, seeking to cultivate the ground organically and grow a wide range of vegetables, including Asian vegetables. The group also keep animals and poultry, as well as undertake experimental work with solar energy.

What has impressed me over the years is not so much the scale or even the success of many of these ventures, for few are large and there are numerous failures. It is that men and women are seeking to get in touch with their roots so that they can not only nurture but learn from the natural world around them. This takes dedication and considerable effort in a consumer-mad world of mass production, synthetic goods and processed foods.

Some Christian groups, not so actively involved on the land, have also taken stewardship very much to heart. Epitomizing this approach is the Life Style movement. It began in 1973 with the now well-known commitment of its members to "live more simply that all of us may simply live". Local Life Style groups exist across the country, such as that in Letchworth. In 1982 this group was meeting fortnightly. It shared meals, discussion and prayers. But it also shared the use of its members' skills, as well as tools, garden equipment and produce, baby clothes and records. "Repair evenings" were held to mend such things as toasters, vacuum cleaners and radios. All this and more, they reported, is "a lot of fun".[8]

Recent years have seen the appearance on the scene of Christians politically committed to the preservation of the planet. In 1981, a Christian Ecology group was founded "to spread ecological insights among Christian people and churches, and to spread Christian insights into the consciousness of the Green Movement".[9] This is a widely scattered network of all denominations, deeply concerned about the survival of the planet. Their aspirations are well summed up by Audrey Bryant:

> The Christian Ecology Group's origins and momentum spring from a sense of great urgency in facing and coming to understand what we people are doing to the earth, given to us by God as our life support, to nourish our bodies, minds and spirits, and mediating to us understandings of God's comprehensive provision, His systems design and His artistry as well as His love. We see repentance as turning from a destructive dominance to a co-operation with God in the earth-systems to which He has linked us in a very close relationship of interdependence. The God who is Love must surely have created all things in love, not only human beings![10]

Christian groups deeply concerned about peace must also be mentioned in this context. They have been on the scene for a long time. Some have roots in the peace movement of the 'thirties, some started just after the last world war on a reconciliation ticket, others arose alongside the Campaign for Nuclear Disarmament in the 'fifties. Most, however, have taken off in the 'eighties, when peacemaking has gathered momentum in a new and dramatic way. Christian C.N.D. is by far the largest Christian body now working in this field, but scores of other groups exist,[11] ranging from groups committed to active but non-violent protest, such as Catholic Peace Action, to those offering mutual support to particular professions campaigning in this field, such as Clergy Against Nuclear Arms.

When only a passing reference can be made to this manifestation of a new catalytic force in the life of the church, it is easy to miss the passion and the power which lies beneath the surface. However, my journeys in the 'seventies and since have made it clear that there was and is still a new quest to share and work in partnership with a Creator God who loves this planet and desires that its potential for life be sustained.

One of the best parables of the search for a deeper understanding and expression of this aspect of the life of the kingdom community is the story of Eirene, the half-built little peace chapel at Molesworth. There, next to the cruise missile base symbolizing man's power to obliterate life, services were held for over a year, until in April of 1986 the bulldozers of the Ministry of Defence razed it to the ground. None the less, worship will continue on the derelict site, to celebrate God's gift of life and to enable all who care to dedicate themselves to be co-stewards with him in the preservation and salvation of the planet.

3. Liberation

There are so many groups to remember – from a large Victorian house outside Inverness being painted and decorated to welcome the first mentally handicapped residents, to a small flat in the centre of Glasgow, inhabited by an idealistic quartet of young Quakers trying to work out how to live communally. From a huge mansion near Exmouth staffed by a Christian group supporting single mothers in need and their children, to a couple of terraced houses between the Falls and the Shankill Road forming the focus of a community working for reconciliation. From a commune near Bristol made up of young Christians providing conference facilities for radical students, to an estate in Dorset given over by its owners to be a home for a large charismatic community with a country-wide preaching and teaching ministry. From a Christian community and wholefood co-operative in the Midlands, to a multi-denominational house group meeting to thrash out issues of faith and life in South London. From a house and smallholding run by a small Christian community providing an opportunity for study and recreation to groups from schools and local churches in Suffolk, to a residential home of healing in the heart of Kent.

These are but a tiny sample of the rich diversity of Christian ventures in community making that I encountered during my travels from the mid-'seventies onwards. Some have faded away. Some have gone from strength to strength. Some have remained fragile plants. But the sheer diversity of opportunities open to Christian men and women, young and old, seeking to work out their own salvation in whatever way they feel called, has greatly impressed me.

If you look through the back copies of the magazine *Community*, this apparently bewildering array of Christian groups and communities is proved to be no mirage. Names like Farncombe, the Quilquox Community, Maranatha, Faith and Light, John Perkins House, Scargill, the Mayola Community, the Columbanus Community, Root Groups, and many more, are probably quite meaningless to the so-called "man in the pew". Yet they represent a kaleidoscope of dynamic cells enabling a wide variety of Christians to be themselves and to express their skills through a wide diversity of ministries, offering support to one another in the process.

This service the institutional church finds it impossible to offer. Grounded as it is in the parochial system and the "gathered congregation", most local churches cannot do more than provide a limited and often narrow range of opportunities through which Christian ministry, lay and ordained, can be exercised. The church is held captive, because it has left its people so few approved vocational options in a pluralistic world now packed with undreamt of opportunities to be and to do.

The plethora of Christian groups and communities which have arisen in recent years accept and rejoice in the fact that Christians, like others, can now choose more freely what they make of their lives. They affirm men and women as they are and where they are; and respect their desire to use their experience and their talents in different ways. This means that men and women are more able to appreciate their uniqueness as persons, that they feel of value, that they can begin to make more sense of the neglected concept of Christian vocation.

The array of groups I encountered during my visits to different parts of the country in the 'seventies and have come across since then is not such a jumble as might at first sight be imagined. There are, broadly speaking, two main categories of groups; those I call "vocational groups", which enable people to pursue a particular cause or form of service, and those I call "support groups" which encourage personal growth or offer personal guidance along the way.

Vocational groups are concerned to affirm the ministry of Christians within either church or society. One or two examples from a wide range must suffice.

The Movement for the Ordination of Women is a group seeking to right what it sees as an injustice within the life of the church. To cite this movement as an example of a "group" coming within the parameters of those to which I have already referred may seem to be stretching the boundaries too far. Yet it is in many ways typical of what is happening, for it defines itself as an organization which "works through local, regional and specialist groups"[12] to achieve its purposes. Formed in 1979, it will end its life when the calling of its members to be priests is affirmed by the Anglican Church in this country. It relies very much on the power of the small Christian cell committed to tackle an issue of contemporary concern.

At the other end of the scale in terms of size and development, is the embryonic Harborne Group. This met for the first time in Birmingham in early 1986. It sprang out of the concern of a number of Methodists, lay and ordained, to promote debate about the future role of their own denomination, left stranded after the failure of unity negotiations, within the wider church and in society.

Another vocational group operating within the church is Church Action with the Unemployed, which came into being in 1982. Its aim is "to encourage and help local churches to do more to assist unemployed people in their own neighbourhoods".[13] Why include it here? I do so because at its heart is a small core group of Christians dedicated to stirring the church as a whole to do more about its response to the world of work, or non-work. I do so, also, because it is a group working very much on the margins and in the cracks, without official backing from the mainstream denominations.

Vocational groups seeking to focus the energies of Christians concerned about the state of society and the world are many more in number. These have come into being to validate and express the calling of Christians to redress what they see as social injustices. Here appear groups involved in such things as race relations and women's rights. There are also groups with a wider brief, though sometimes these find it more difficult to sustain the enthusiasm of their members. One such is the recently formed Christians in Politics, "a national network of individuals and local groups"[14], many recently students, attempting to "provide a Christian forum for debate on the complex issues arising from political activity".

Another large section of vocational Christian groups is engaged in some form of caring ministry. As well known as any here are the l'Arche houses. These were first set up in France and provided "communes where mentally handicapped people and those society calls 'normal', can live and work together, growing towards freedom in an atmosphere of love and respect".[15] In this country there are now thirteen such houses located as far apart as Sussex and Inverness.

A more modest endeavour is Crossline, typical of many Christian groups involved in a counselling ministry, which consists of a team which began work in Plymouth in 1974. It offers assistance to those facing personal crises, a listening ear to those wanting to talk, longer-term help through friendship groups, and social education programmes in schools.

Far and away the smallest number of vocational Christian groups is involved in the mainstream organizations and institutions of our society. There are a few more established and formalized Christian bodies linking teachers engaged in religious education in schools. There have also been attempts to establish evangelical associations to gather Christians working as nurses, policemen, social workers, businessmen and so on, in particular for prayer and bible study. But the new generation of Christian cells, about which I am writing here, has not yet penetrated this important sphere in any significant way, despite moves in a few quarters, such as further education, the arts and community work. It is a sphere of lay vocation so important that if it continues to remain neglected or forgotten by those seeking the coming of the kingdom community, the journey towards the latter is going to be a very slow one indeed.

A second main category is that of Christian support groups. These are made up of those attempting to encourage personal development and to offer personal guidance along the way. This need always overlaps with that of those looking for the kind of vocational opportunity just mentioned, but in some groups it is given especial attention.

This is particularly the case with the community house. There are probably some thirty or forty of these scattered around the country at the moment, excluding those with a specialist function, like the l'Arche houses. Typical here might be the Beeston Community House in Nottingham. This was set up in 1975 and has developed its own distinctive pattern of life since then. It consists of half-a-dozen or so residents who stay for periods averaging two to three years. Most are in the twenty to twenty-five age group and single, between finishing college and starting on a career. They meet each week for communion, and every month for a community meal and community meeting. To these events the "extended community" of non-resident friends is welcome. The residents help to support a community worker operating in Beeston. The house has become a focus for the ecumenical life of the area and now produces the Beeston churches' newsletter.

One other kind of group which has the affirmation and support of individuals as its primary task is the house group. The sort of group to which I refer here is not the typical Lent group or bible study fellowship, but more akin to that in which Sue and I were involved for six years here in Birmingham. This consisted of half a dozen couples who met once a month to have supper together and to talk over a wide range of concerns, ranging from questions of faith to how to handle our family budgets. Occasionally we had social outings with the children or a weekend away together.

The group gave us the opportunity to explore where we as individuals, and not just as couples, were in our search for faith and fulfilment. We were able to share our problems at considerable depth and to guide and support each other through some difficult patches. Towards the end of the group's life, we each spent an evening telling our life story in any way we wanted, and received the group's reflections on our present situation and possible "next steps". In many cases it deepened our awareness of possibilities as yet un-realized.

The affirmation of their members by Christian cells, be the group concerned more with vocation or support, is an essential beginning in the process of liberation. The group here fulfils a function which in other contexts the family and the institutional church seek to fulfil – in the latter case, as I have suggested, very inadequately. The groups I have en-countered "re-present" Christ to their members, and affirm them in his name by deed as well as word. At the same time, they seek as part of "the priesthood of all believers" to open up to their number a new awareness of what personal fulfilment and wholeness might mean.

Thus all the groups I have met are also engaged in the process of awareness raising. They offer a rich panorama of possibilities, some stressing the inner and some the outer search. These twin poles of the quest for salvation are well summed up in the aspirations of a still very young association in the north-east called the Lindisfarne Network. It is committed to furthering the "Journey In-ward, Journey Outward", a search by its members for an answer to "the question of what their life is for [and] what is the unique contribution to the life of the world that God is calling them to make at this stage in their life".[16]

Vocational groups encourage this quest for fulfilment through the wide variety of outgoing ministries to which I have already referred. Support groups provide help with the inward aspect of the journey. Amongst the latter are a range of groups exploring new forms of Christian spirituality, such as the Mayola Community in Bedfordshire, which is made up of a dozen or so people living near to one another.

A daily office said by those available on weekdays, in a specially built house extension used as a quiet room, is complemented by members' personal prayers, with an emphasis on meditative and contemplative prayer. This is backed up by study and creative activity, from craftwork to preaching, together with an economical lifestyle of sharing. On a national level the Julian Meetings, which began in 1973 and now number about 150,[17] are small ecumenical groups which seek to foster the practice and teaching of contemplative prayer. A typical meeting consists of a short reading which leads into a period of silence lasting twenty minutes or more. This will be followed by discussion, and then a time to chat informally and have coffee. They are minimally organized but have as their aim the provision of an enriching spirituality for ordinary Christians in their everyday lives. Offering a different approach to the same quest is the Creative Arts Network which began in 1980. It is a loose-knit association of people helping Christians across the country to explore theology, spirituality and lifestyle through painting, clay, writing, music and drama, in order to realize "their enormous potential for learning, growth and sheer enjoyment".[18]

This inward journey is also sustained by groups concerned to minister to those facing mental or spiritual breakdown. For some years the trail-blazer here was the Clinical Theology Association, which set out to train people in pastoral care for the promotion of "the deepening of Christian life and growth towards personal maturity and stability".[19] Similar forms of pastoral care have now been taken further by such places as Heronbrook, "a house of affirmation" in a delightful country setting near Knowle in Warwickshire. I have visited it on numerous occasions and have been greatly impressed not just by the beauty and tranquillity of the place but by the ever courteous and kindly welcome. It was established in 1978 by Sister Malachy Joseph Lynch, then Superior General of the Sisters of Charity of St Paul, herself a psychologist. Heronbrook offers counselling skills and the support of a therapeutic community to those ordained and to members of the religious orders passing through a period of personal stress. Its focus is "on self-understanding and insight-building"[20] to enable those in need to work through the meaning of their humanity in today's world. Through the help of Heronbrook many have been able to fulfil themselves in creative ministries across the globe. Though there are a number of other counselling centres serving a similar clientele scattered across the country, many more addressed particularly to the mental and spiritual needs of the laity are urgently required.

The journey towards personal fulfilment which the new generation of Christian groups facilitates is not simply a matter of affirmation and awareness raising. It is also about calling men and women to account in the name of Christ. It is important to note here that it is the group as such which calls its members to account, with no one person figuring more prominently than another in that process. It is also to the group and its ministry, as "re-presenting" Christ and his kingdom commuity, that members offer themselves.

With many groups this call and commitment are not formalized. Margaret Potts, writing of St Julian's, states that "membership of the community involves a vocation to a way of life rather than submission to a new race".[21] The Community of Celebration saw their well-regulated mode of living as itself synonymous with a religious rule of life. A house group in Sheffield, originating in the mid-'seventies out of the survivors of three local Lent groups, sees call and commitment in terms of a fortnightly meeting, of seeking a deeper prayer life and of mutual support. They write, "We have developed a very strong sense of concern for each other and know ourselves to be 'brothers and sisters in Christ', who *want* to support each other and understand each other's struggles. We work at getting to know, trust and love one another."[22]

For other groups call and commitment are more explicitly defined. Before One for Christian Renewal came into existence in 1970, its instigators spent a long while hammering out its "declaration":

> As members of a world in revolution, a divided church, a generation for which forgiveness and love alone have authority, we commit ourselves
>
> to accept one another in Christ
>
> to study together the nature of our responsibility for God's world
>
> to combat poverty, racialism and oppression through social and political action.
>
> to help in re-creating the one church – new in witness, worship and life
>
> to support actively those doing the work of Christ inside or outside the institutional church
>
> to ground the action for renewal in our own situation
>
> to underwrite this commitment financially.[23]

The Grail, a Roman Catholic lay women's community in Middlesex, set their own more formal commitment in this particularly impressive context:

> Our basic purpose is to help ourselves and other people towards true growth and freedom. This means living a full Christian life ourselves and as a group; striving to become a working model of what Christian community could be: a community that exists not just for itself but for others . . . It involves us in the breaking down of

barriers between people generally, between clergy and laity, between classes and cultures. And this process includes in its dynamism healing, the building of bridges, and building communion . . . It calls us to accept our responsibility for the world, for helping to transform it into a world of peace and fellowship; for making Christ present and active wherever we live and work, and in so doing to see the value of all created realities and, supremely, the value of the human person. In a word, it calls us to take our share in extending the work of Christ, in making all things new.[24]

More recently, Cornerstone, the mixed Roman Catholic and Protestant community in Belfast, has given overt expression to the call and commitment of its members in the following words:

Today we are broken, we are needing, we do not feel one people. But we resolve to listen with our living God, to walk where we can, knowing He will lead us where we cannot at the moment go. We resolve to listen, pray and wait, sharing with each other the vision He is giving us.

We want to bind ourselves to each other and to His promise through a simple commitment in love – to hold each other constantly in our hearts before the Father; to intercede together with each other for our people, re-membering particularly the hour between eleven and twelve each day and night.

We will take the Beatitudes as our guide for our desire to live a Gospel way of life; offering by our lives that special quality of merciful love best described in the original Hebrew words, *Hesed, Rahamin* – that quality of love which was the fruit of the Covenant.

While this is always before us, never accomplished, we recognize that we will continue to hunger and thirst for justice, for wholeness, for true peace for all our people.

And as some among us, together with others, go a step further and live together, or nearby, in these districts, we will do all we can to encourage, discern with, and support such moves.

We entrust our future steps into the Hands of the Living God, in whom we live and move and have our being.[25]

Yet such groups cannot be all things to all people. They have the responsibility of affirming, nurturing and calling their members to account, but only so that they can be liberated to fulfil themselves in the wider service of Christ, whose service is perfect freedom. Most know that personal growth, both inward and outward, takes place within, but also beyond any one group. Unlike so much in the institutional church, the new generation of Christian groups is learning to release and not to imprison its members.

I have met many women and men who have experienced the joy of liberation and salvation, autonomy and wholeness, through the new generation of Christian groups and communities. I have met many for whom life has been transformed and shown to offer possibilities beyond their wildest dreams. There are those known to very few, tilling the land, working for peace, serving the needy, striving for justice, or just saying their prayers, from the wilds of Scotland to the East End of London. There are those now internationally famous for their witness to the liberating grace of Christ. Here I refer to three of the latter group, Jean Vanier, Rosemary Haughton and Jim Wallis, because between them they seem to me to represent that freedom and fulfilment in Christ that many are seeking. All three were speakers at the first ever National Community Congress of Christian groups held in the United Kingdom at Birmingham in 1980.

Jean Vanier is the founder of the worldwide network of l'Arche community houses for the mentally handicapped. The rich insights he has gained through this work have made him a person of great spiritual stature, as well as one who has helped thousands to gain a deeper understanding of the meaning of being human. At the 1980 Community Congress, summing up his own experiences as well as addressing all of us, he said:

> To be able to accept that we are often sinful people but also that we have gifts and are loved by God, we have strengths – that is the beginning of human wisdom. Accepting one's darkness and hoping to grow to greater light is a lifetime's work. But it can only commence as we begin to really accept ourselves as we are, with our wounds; not with a morbid, depressive acceptance but filled with hope, because this is what we are. It's no use pretending that we can grow unless we grow from what we are. If darkness and powers of hate are in me, this is what I am. I can learn to grow from that. Then I can walk with others towards wholeness, gradually beginning truly to love the broken part within me, and I can begin to love the broken parts in other people. So it is that I will really begin to accept people as they are, without judging, and learn to become a peacemaker, somebody who is prepared to serve people in their brokenness.[26]

Rosemary Haughton is best known for her many books on the Christian life, especially in connection with personal relationships. She is less well known for the way in which in 1974 she, her family and friends set about the creation of the Lothlorien Community in the countryside of Kirkcudbrightshire. This community is now well established and, amongst other things, offers support to a small number of those suffering from mental or emotional illnesses. She has constantly striven to point us to the still suppressed and disastrously neglected power of the feminine in human development, personal and corporate. She now spends a good deal of time in the United States seeking to encourage the formation of small Christian groups which will witness to the centrality of prayer and express an active concern for the poor and disadvantaged.

At the 1980 Congress she reminded us of the danger of getting stuck, because "community" becomes too cherished an ideal:

> There is a real danger of smugness, of feeling we've found a way to live which really makes sense. And it will be true. If we've tried very hard to live according to really human values, gospel values, and somehow it's working, then it's true to say that this does make sense. Yet in that statement there's a temptation to feel that's fine; now all we have to do is to go on doing it. But the point of doing it is to be available to the power of divine love so that it can keep breaking through into the world. Any feeling that we've got that we're okay is going to make that very difficult because we're crossing over from the camp of the sinners to the camp of the righteous and, as soon as we know ourselves righteous, we're pretty well armoured against God. So we need, as vulnerable and unimportant groups, to be aware that that's what we have to be. We shall have to go on being upset. We shall have to go on finding that our plans come to nothing. We shall need to go on having to let go.[27]

Jim Wallis is one of the founder members of Sojourners, a community set up in inner-city Washington, D.C. It is based on evangelical principles, is dedicated to the alleviation of poverty and injustice, and to challenging the insanity of the nuclear arms race. Jim Wallis has fulfilled his own calling in Christ through a ministry dedicated to a passionate proclamation of a radical faith as the condition for the salvation of both the individual and the world. At the 1980 Congress, he spoke of his conviction that only those liberated by Christ can be genuine peacemakers:

> Most of us are not free enough yet to be peacemakers. Our faith is not operational enough yet to break the grip of the whole of the war system on our lives and on our communities. Peacemaking requires a maturity in our spiritual life that most of us have yet to experience. The Christian community can be a place that teaches and breeds that kind of maturity of faith. Community can become, in effect, a training school, a training ground for peacemakers, because community can teach us things that make for peace while exposing those things that make for war. Only in community can we really experience dealing with conflict and prejudice and fear and hostility. It is there where we can be put in touch with our sin, put in touch with our propensity towards violence, where we learn the ways of resolving conflict, of absorbing anguish and aggression, of overcoming prejudice, of healing our fear, of being reconciled to our enemies. Only that kind of reconciliation, created and established among very ordinary people, will put us in a position to extend peace into the public arena. Community is that arena where security and insecurity, enmity and reconciliation, play themselves out, are given free rein, so that people can be healed, so that they might be redeemed, so that we might finally be peacemakers.[28]

These three speakers were pointing to the profound importance of kingdom community groups as a place of preparation for life and living. But they were also saying that community is created within each person who has been affirmed, made aware and liberated by Christ. Such liberation brings with it the responsibility and resources to be servants and heralds of the kingdom community even when we are isolated or persecuted.

Though such groups are engaged in a host of affirming and awareness-raising ministries, calling all men and women to make the utmost of their lives, and seeking to bring them to a liberating and saving faith in Christ, there is special concern for the vulnerable, the disadvantaged and the marginalized. Thus many groups, some of which I have already mentioned, are working with the unemployed, the homeless, alcoholics, the mentally ill, the physically handicapped, the elderly and infirm, and the dying.

This "option for the vulnerable" is seen as powerfully as anywhere in the work of Helen House, a hospice in Oxford opened in 1982, for children with life-threatening illnesses. The inspiration of Mother Frances, an Anglican sister, it is now staffed and supported by a team of religious and lay people whose common concern is that children in acute need should find as much happiness and fulfilment as is possible. Within this "home of healing", in the deepest sense of the term, are brought together the fit and the ill, the old and the young, the mature and the beginners, to be one small but potent sign of that liberation from fear, despair and the power of death, which opens up the way to the kingdom community.

4. Unity

We tend very easily to talk about community, but in fact the community thing comes out of the Christian. The call to follow Christ is the call to community, because it's in each other and with each other that we discover the presence of Christ. So we begin by trying to follow, and very often that's a lonely experience, which sounds paradoxical. That moment of letting go, of being willing to take risks and just set out, no matter what anybody else thinks, is very lonely. But it's in that following that we encounter each other, recognize other people on the same journey and discover what Christian community is; in fact what the church is.[29]

With these words Rosemary Haughton finished her address to the 1980 Congress. She was not just speaking for herself but for many listening to her; those who had set out in search of individual salvation and found it to be intimately bound up with the salvation of everyone else. The fulfilment of each one of us is an integral part of the fulfilment of every one of us.

That has been the experience of Taena, a small farming community at Upton St Leonards in Gloucestershire. Taena began in 1941 as an agnostic group of left-wing pacifists. In 1950, after a period of deep heart-seaching, its members chose to become Roman Catholic. Ten years later, the community felt the time had come to loosen their common commitment and opted for a more pluralistic economic and religious lifestyle. They are still living together in a loose association of households today.

Taena has plumbed the depths and heights of corporate living and been greatly enriched by its journey. George Ineson, one of the founders, speaks of what he calls "holding the circle" as profoundly important in this process of growth:

This means to contain the opposites, to let the opposites meet so that the new can be conceived and the new life cared for and protected within the circle. The opposites are inner and outer, each reflecting the other – aloneness and togetherness. Whatever the difficulties are, a solution will emerge if you can contain the problem and live through it. Once the community divides into two or more separate organisms, the heat escapes and the meal is uncooked – leaving only partial surface solutions instead of a radical transformation. Living in a town or city offers so many possibilities of escape that it is hardly possible to contain a problem in this way except in the limited sphere of the family; this is one reason why so many of us today never pass beyond adolescence, the spirit imprisoned in a surface adaptation to a particular external context.[30]

The new generation of Christians seeking out the corporate nature of the kingdom community is taking up that challenge.

The Grail has been a pioneer in work with Roman Catholic families. It has encouraged the formation of "family circles", groups of six or eight couples who are or have been in some way associated with the Grail, which generally meet monthly for a meal, discussion, prayer and fun. The circles vary from loose-knit to very close-knit, from the involvement of couples to that of all the family. More recently, the Grail has been thinking more in terms of a "family network", which enables each family to keep in touch to the extent and in the way it wishes. To facilitate the sharing of experiences there are "family days", "family weekends" and "family weeks" for those wanting to spend time or holiday together.

In Hackney, East London, is the Family Tree Community, typical of a number of attempts by younger Christians to live life well together. It has never had more than five permanent members but has existed for eight years, sharing space, meals and material good as well as daily prayers. The community has seen the hospitality offered to many visitors as a major focus of its ministry. It has also given support to a nearby day centre for handicapped children and to local churches. "Anything we do as a community", comments Tim Powell, "needs to grow from the centrality of Jesus in our lives, for there is no point in undertaking anything unless it is in some way furthering his kingdom."[31]

In Oxford there has existed for some years a quite different kind of group, yet just as closely bound together by their search for the kingdom. The Oxford Covenant Community is a group of half-a-dozen women who meet "to support and affirm women as real followers of Christ", to discuss feminist books or articles, to work for peace and justice, to pray and worship together, and to assist one another in a variety of ministries ranging from preaching to running a women's information centre. Such activities, they write, were "the outcome of a growing feeling of community and have in turn provided a new and stronger basis for our community".[32]

These groups are a tiny fraction of those who, through their life or work together, have discovered something of the true meaning of the fellowship of the Holy Spirit. Many have, at least initially, been drawn to share with those of similar religious or social backgrounds. Others have deliberately set out to cross such boundaries – a vocation which becomes more than a gesture in a situation like that of Northern Ireland.

In 1983, the Columbanus Community set up house in Belfast as a deliberate attempt to "witness to the belief that in Christ, through the power of the Spirit, two opposing nations in Ireland can learn to live and work together".[33] The membership consists of Roman Catholics and Protestants who share a daily eucharist. They pool material goods and commit themselves to a simple rule of life. Their ministry is one of hospitality, as well as a variety of social and pastoral work in the locality.

The Corrymeela Community exercises a similar but wider ministry of reconciliation and unity. Its Ballycastle Centre provides a meeting place for a host of groups, ranging from youth clubs to widows' associations, from meetings of members of the helping professions to conferences on such themes as "Breaking down the enmity" and "Faith and politics". There are special gatherings for young adults. Every second year a major "Summerfest" is held. In 1985 this was attended by some eight hundred people, with many more day visitors, and took the theme of "The Upside Down Kingdom" (the Beatitudes). This was explored across the religious divide through key speakers, workshops, music, drama, arts and crafts and social events. In Belfast and in other towns, as already noted, Corrymeela groups meet and engage in local peacemaking initiatives in a variety of ways.

Operating in a very different situation is Handsworth Breakthrough in Birmingham. Here a small group of Christians has set up a company to employ young people, organize public events and publish records and booklets. One of its chief concerns is to enable the various local (and mainly black) churches to work together on projects of communal value. Through visits, slide-shows, concerts and workshops, it also seeks to bring suburban churches to a greater awareness of the problems and potential of the inner city.

Christians Together was launched in 1983 after the failure of the "Covenant" proposals, in the conviction that "God was still calling us to pursue the vision of unity, though the way ahead was unclear".[34] It has held conferences (three for theological students), publishes a newsletter, and seeks to promote reflection and action related to unity at both national and local levels. Its members undertake to pray for unity on the tenth day of each month.

Praying for unity is a central concern of the Farncombe Community. This is a small group of women living communally near Godalming. It began life in 1964 as "a fellowship of prayer for unity",[35] and since then has remained faithful to this particular ministry. To Farncombe belong both "companions" and "members of the fellowship" who, though scattered across the country, pledge themselves regularly to pray that all Christians may come into a deeper experience of the unity of the Holy Spirit.

The search for a deeper awareness and expression of unity is also being pursued by an increasing number of Christian groups in relation to those of other faiths. Two very different expressions of this concern are Seva Sadan (meaning "house of friendship") and the Multi-Faith Resource Unit, both located in Birmingham. The former began in 1971 in inner-city Sparkhill, to provide language teaching, an advice service, cultural activities and pastoral care to the Gujerati community living round about. The house has usually had a core community of three, with members drawn from its sponsoring bodies, the Irish Presbyterian, the United Reform Chruch and the Church of North India (an Asian Christian).

The Multi-Faith Resource Unit started in 1982. It is a Christian initiative but has moved to embrace those of other faiths in its core group. Its aim is to enable those of different religious traditions to work together on cultural programmes which further interfaith dialogue and understanding in ways which can widen horizons and bring new insights. It is concerned not so much about the outcome as the quality of dialogue, and seeks to promote open encounter and exchange both in Birmingham and other parts of the country.

Another notable category of Christian groups working for the wholeness of the kingdom community are those which put themselves alongside the economically or socially marginalized. This was the purpose of Bystock Court, set up in 1965, where a core Christian group for many years provided a caring community for women, and sometimes their children, at a point of major crisis in their lives. The ethos of this venture (now ended) was well summed up by the words on the wall facing you when first entering it:

And the Lord said –

"Behold I have set aside this house, and have blessed it,
That it may be a refuge for the weary.
Peace is to be found within its walls,
And friendship.
All who cross the threshold shall find welcome,
And a comforting hand to give fresh courage
In place of dark despair.
In this house shall My Name be glorified,
For that which is shattered
Shall be made whole."[36]

With a similar concern are the l'Arche houses for the mentally handicapped. My own visits to these have always been occasions of fascination and enjoyment. They are places where the helpers and the handicapped seem to establish mutual relationships of respect and affection, with many lasting friendships emerging. For me, the fellowship of these homes is typified by one evening meal I was privileged to share in the l'Arche house in Liverpool, during which I have rarely laughed so much. I left feeling that, unlike my companions that night, it is many of us who are not called "handicapped" who have forgotten the art of living and loving.

Despite the impressive caring ministry of many new Christian groups, there still remain social divisions to be overcome, not least that of class. Some groups, like the Community of Christ the King, situated in a multi-racial area of Leicester and involved in counselling and work with young offenders, would see themselves as more working- than middle-class. But by and large, the church's loss of contact with the underprivileged, not least during the Industrial Revolution, has deprived even the community movement of participants from this section of the population. Thus to demonstrate to those from the working class, or growing "under class", that the coming of the kingdom is as vital to them, materially and spiritually, as to anyone else is a formidable task ahead.

Yet if the recent generation of Christian groups are not *of* the poor, many are at least seeking to stand *with* them. This is especially the case with groups which direct their energies to confront the injustices of our society, such as Church Action on Poverty. This began in 1982 and now has some thousand members. It seeks to challenge government policies, through papers, consultations and an information and news folder, on such issues as the housing crisis, low pay, the future of the Welfare State and the work of the Manpower Services Commission. It has a number of regional groups which run their own programmes, though these have been harder to establish.

This overview of a handful of the many groups I have encountered, and which are seeking to make manifest the unity of the Holy Spirit, can only offer a glimpse of what is happening on the margins or within the cracks of the institutional church. I have made no reference to scores of other pioneering ventures working for reconciliation and unity – the Association of Interchurch Families, the Hengrave Hall Community, the International Ecumenical Fellowship, the Daily Bread Co-operative, St Basil's Project, the Campaign Against Racism and Fascism, the Zebra Project, and numerous interfaith groups, to name but a few.[37] Although the particular ministries of these groups differ considerably, each is saying a bold "Yes" to life together. Each in its own way is seeking to give expression to the fellowship of the kingdom community.

All such groups are aware that this quest for the unity of the Spirit challenges as well as guides their work. The journey is not just about caring and co-operation, but about dealing with deep enmity and bitter conflict. It is about facing corporate issues of justice and reconciliation, as well as personal questions of human relationships. Thus many groups face the need to make some form of public declaration, in word or deed, of their "option for the poor", and not simply a noise off-stage.

Few are finding their vocation easy to fulfil. Few have failed to encounter the challenges of healing themselves if they are to heal the world. None have found that the quest for unity can only be either an internal or an external affair. But many of them, despite formidable obstacles, have become signs of the kingdom community.

5. Networking

"i thank You God for most this amazing
day: for leaping greenly spirits of trees
and a blue true dream of sky; and everything
which is natural which is infinite which is yes

(i who died am alive again today,
and this is the sun's birthday; this is the
birth day of life and of love and wings: and of
the gay great happening illimitably earth)

how should tasting touching hearing seeing
breathing any – lifted from the no
of all nothing – human merely being
doubt unimaginable You?

(now the ears of my ears awake and
now the eyes of my eyes are opened)"[38]

This book is about people saying yes – to themselves, to their fellows, to life, to God. And not just saying it but living out to the full what it means in everyday events and relationships. Many in our impersonal technological society have given up or "died", but those of whom I have written are "alive again today" and celebrate "the sun's birthday".[39]

I wrote these words in 1977, at the end of a book about the groups and communities I had visited over the preceding years. What excited me then, and still excites me today, was the passionate "Yes" to life they were saying – some loud and broadcast widely, some whispered and spoken to only a few – through their lives and through their work.

This "Yes" to life was in response to the vitality and beauty of the planet earth and to God the Life-giver, the Creator and the Preserver. This meant not just joy in and celebration of the wonders of creation, but a commitment to defend a planet that was threatened, be it by the depletion of its resources, pollution or nuclear war. It was a commitment to be good stewards of the natural world entrusted to them and to bringing all life to fulfilment and wholeness.

It was a "Yes" to life in reponse to the uniqueness and value of each person and to the freedom offered by Christ the Liberator. This meant groups giving their members every opportunity to grow to maturity as human beings and utilize to the full the talent and skills given to them. It meant a determination to ensure that each and every person could find freedom and fulfilment, whatever their condition or situation, physical, mental or spiritual.

It was a "Yes" to life in response to the privilege of being members of the human race and to the unifying power of the Holy Spirit. This I found in the readiness of groups to be open to one another and to seek a creative intimacy, as well as to work for the ending of the barriers that caused death-dealing division and violence.

As I visited, met, talked to and observed this kaleidoscope of groups, I came to see their "Yes" to life, to liberation and to unity as hallmarks of the kingdom community being expressed in a way which enabled people to see what that community could be "on earth as in heaven".

If the message of the kingdom community was one of life,

liberation and unity, its form was a web of small dynamic cells characterized by distinctiveness within corporateness, diversity within togetherness. It was a human scale community which affirmed and encouraged those seeking to fulfil themselves as unique persons, yet one which recognized and sought to strengthen the brotherhood and sisterhood of all. Thus the interdependence of each and every one had to be fully acknowledged. Nothing less was worthy of the depth and breadth of life within the kingdom community and of the dynamic wholeness it offered.

For the groups I met, the search for this kingdom community was seen as an exhilarating journey. It required a vigorous sharing and exchange of life quite untypical of what went on in the institutions of the modern world, the church included. Yet it was also a costly journey. In 1977, I drew attention to the toll it took of human energy and resilience "to sustain the emotional demands in every intentional community of living cheek-by-jowl with those whose habits and attitudes differ greatly from one's own; to endure cold, rain, and mud at Keveral Farm and Lothlorien; to cope with hard manual work at Pilsdon and Scoraig; to take the wear and tear of being on hand to deal with the needs of broken families at Bystock Court, of the homeless in the Cyrenian shelters, and of those disoriented by violence at Corrymeela."[40] Such a journey of necessity demanded wholehearted commitment and determination. But it also required a sense of purpose and strength often well beyond that which was humanly possible.

This journey, I believe, was one inspired and guided by the Holy Trinity offering life, liberation and unity as a gift and opportunity. Through the down-to-earth search of these groups the divine life of the Trinity, as symbol, model, example, and catalyst of the kingdom community, was made manifest. They were building a community empowered not only by men and women working out their own salvation, but by the presence within that process, also at great cost, of Father, Son and Holy Spirit.

The groups I encountered were convinced that their vision of the kingdom community, albeit partial, could not just be talked about; it had to be earthed. This was no holiday for those wanting to "escape" from the fray. On the coming of the kingdom community depended the life or death of our world, our society and every person within it. It was a divine imperative that Christian men and women gave their all to create signs of the kingdom, however small, so that others could see, believe and live.

It was also crucial that the whole church, herald and servant of the kingdom, recognized those signs and obeyed the call to follow where they pointed, though the changes required of it en route would be profound and long-lasting; not least because the vision of the kingdom community espoused by Christian groups turned the values and structures of the church as institution on their head. For these groups the kingdom was about life, liberation and unity, not about passivity, dependence and division. It was about pride of place being given to the threatened, the vulnerable and the poor, not about possessions, power and privilege. The kingdom was about a rich pluriformity and diversity of Christian ministries, not about uniformity and a restrictive clerical/lay division of labour. It was about a creative and cohesive interdependence, not about a dull and aloof parallelism. It was about commitment to the journey, not about nominal church membership. The kingdom community was about a gospel which inspired through engagement and exchange; not about pronouncements from on high or from afar.

But how were the groups I encountered actually faring in blazing a trail towards this vision of the kingdom community? Were they persuading the church to pause, take its bearings again, and opt for life rather than senility and death?

Through their own being and work most groups were clearly and impressively speaking their "Yes" to life. In themselves most groups appeared vitally alive and bearing witness to one or other facet of the kingdom community. Yet there were problems. On the one hand, there was the danger that any group on its own could become too homogeneous in lifestyle or concerns to do justice to the rich pluriformity of the kingdom community. In this case its very distinctiveness, and thus the means of offering liberation and autonomy to its members, could be restrictive. On the other hand, across all groups there was the danger of too weak a sense of togetherness to give the inspiration and strength necessary to facilitate the emergence of that prophetic movement of regeneration which I felt the institutional church urgently needed.

My conviction that a kingdom community movement, corporate and identifiable, was now a divine imperative had been borne out by my experience of the captivity of the church in Sheffield and London. It had grown stronger as I saw the prophetic potential of the groups I visited after leaving London. It was given further reinforcement from a quarter which hitherto I had known little about, the appearance of so-called "basic ecclesial communities" on the Latin American scene.

As I learnt more about the fascinating story of the growth of these communities in many South American countries I was excited and impressed. At the same time, I realized that there were important differences between them and what I now (and shall henceforth) call "basic Christian groups" on the United Kingdom scene,[41] not least the predominance within the former of the very poor and of Roman Catholics. None the less, I remained sure that our basic Christian groups shared one fundamental characteristic with the Latin American communities; they were both part of a growing movement across the world in search of the kingdom community, and of new and dynamic forms for the church as its servant. What mattered was not so much from where those in Latin America or the United Kingdom started, which would inevitably be influenced by history, culture and politics, but where they were heading. Thus I saw all such groups in Latin America or the United Kingdom as an integral part of a prophetic and profoundly important kingdom community movement.

Even so, much remained to be done. In the 'seventies the community movement in this country was a young plant. Most groups were not only struggling to take root and survive, but as yet had little awareness that they might be part of a divine process essential to the re-creation of the church and the transformation of society. I believed that my work at this time was, therefore, to help raise that awareness and help bring to birth in this country a movement which could face the formidable journey ahead, as well as sustain itself in the process.

The possibility of an identifiable and purposeful movement emerging with any rapidity was remote. Not only was a wider vision lacking, but contact and communication were minimal. An exciting exchange of life went on within groups but infrequently between them. Nor was I ready to play a role which might have speeded up the process in the short-term, yet hindered the growth of a more self-reliant and resilient movement in the long-term. The network had to precede the movement.

"Networks" and "networking" are now terms used in everyday parlance. They were not so common in the mid-'seventies. However, in the book I wrote in 1977, I drew attention to the idea of the network and included a penultimate chapter about it.[42] The network has blossomed as a social form for two main reasons: the emergence of rapid and global means of communication and, for many, a feeling that it might provide a human yet open form of organization midway between the narrow intimacy of the small group and the efficiency, but impersonality, of the large institution.[43]

Those writing about networks pick out five essential characteristics. Networks need a "spider" to maintain them.

They need a regular bulletin or newsletter. They need a central contact point. They need a list of the names of those linked in to them. They need occasional local get-togethers. And they also need very occasional gatherings of all, or as many as possible, of those involved.[44]

For establishing and maintaining a network of Christian groups and communities, the first two requirements already existed from the mid-'seventies onwards. I was able to be a kind of "spider" (though "fly on the wall" might have been a more appropriate designation). A bulletin was already in being in the form of the *Community* magazine.

The next item on the agenda seemed to be some national contact point, and this came into being early in 1977, in part because my family became tired of our house being cluttered up with the mass of papers and leaflets I had collected during my travels. A young couple in Birmingham, very interested in the community movement, kindly agreed both to provide a home for these papers in their front-room, and to assist any enquirers who 'phoned or called. A year later they moved away, and Westhill College, where I was by now lecturing, offered rooms on the campus to accommodate the material. We appointed a part-time Resources Officer, Valerie Knight, who has since then answered hundreds of enquiries with thoughtfulness and patience. The unit was called "The Community Resources Centre".

No comprehensive list of groups existed until I added one to the back of my book in 1977.[45] In 1980, the first ever *Directory of Christian Communities and Groups*[46] was published by the Community Resources Centre, containing names, addresses and notes describing some four hundred basic Christian groups and religious orders within the United Kingdom.

To persuade very busy or economically struggling groups to spare the time and expense to meet together was a more formidable, yet just as vital, task, if networking were to progress and the emergence of the community movement be fostered.

The first gathering of this kind came in 1975 at Harborne Hall, Birmingham.[47] Some fifty people attended. I recall only two things about the weekend. One was the exciting variety of groups represented – from the Focolare to the Grubb Institute, from Taena to the Student Christian Movement, from the Community of Celebration to Lee Abbey. The other was the sense of a deep common bond which became evident on the first Friday evening as we slowly went round the room telling our stories and sharing our hopes. At Harborne Hall I first came really to appreciate the rich diversity and dynamic interdependence which are at the heart of the kingdom community.

Two years later, another gathering of groups was held, this time at Hengrave Hall in Suffolk.[48] The experience was as powerful as ever, and has remained so every time I have been present at this kind of conference. Once again our Friday evening sharing created a feeling of corporate hope as we sensed ourselves to be engaged in a common search for a re-created church and a transformed world. "I left Hengrave thanking God that I have been born right now and not a century ago", wrote one participant to me afterwards.

Hengrave Hall was notable for one other occurrence. For the first time we were joined by members of the religious orders. This was in part due to the vision of Alan Harrison, then Secretary of the Advisory Council for (Anglican) Religious Communities, who had come to see that the religious had a great deal in common with the Christian community movement. A year before he had written about "missing links"[49] between the older and younger Christian groups, and was instrumental in encouraging both Anglican and Roman Catholic religious to be present at Hengrave.

This new connection was a vital one. On the one hand, it meant that many of the younger and less stable groups could draw on the considerable experience of community building present within the religious orders. On the other hand, the latter could test their current lifestyle and apostolate against the vision and imaginative experimentation of younger groups. It was the beginning of a very fruitful exchange of experience and ideas which has gone on ever since.

At Hengrave Hall, a view was expressed that small conferences, though useful, were not enough. A larger gathering, the occasional major symbolic event to keep all networks alive, was needed. So we set about the long and arduous task of organizing the first national Congress of basic Christian groups ever to be held in the United Kingdom. This eventually took place over five hectic days in September 1980, on the campuses of Woodbrooke and Westhill Colleges in Birmingham.[50] It was attended by some two hundred and fifty people, representing a hundred and six basic Christian groups and religious orders (thirteen Anglican and twenty-nine Roman Catholic). Though our three main speakers, Jean Vanier, Rosemary Haughton and Jim Wallis, were excellent, it was the meeting and talking with those on the same journey which made it such a memorable gathering. Three comments from participants must suffice to sum up the overall feel of what was far more a "happening" than a run-of-the-mill conference:

> The Congress opened my eyes to the extent of what you call the alternative church. It is most encouraging to know just how many Christians are being called to valid ministry outside the parish.

> A living experience of the dynamic work of the Holy Spirit in the world. A challenging experience of what it means to be a Christian in the world today. A rewarding experience of meeting up with so many marvellous people. An enriching experience which I hope will become fruitful in the years ahead.

Loved meeting all the "rainbow" of different Christian communities and individuals. Longing for something more "concrete" to emerge but I think the Holy Spirit's doing it all the time! This network is helping to bring in God's kingdom and root it here on earth.[51]

I carried away from this Congress two especially vivid memories. The first was the sheer exhilaration of seeing so many people – most of whom I had only encountered before, if at all, in ones or twos – gathered together in a diverse but single company to share their experiences and hopes. The sight of so many people, deeply dedicated to the coming of the kingdom community, at long last assembled together, at one point moved me to tears. I felt that even if I could do little more to help this remarkable company on its way, the reality that they symbolized and the source of power on which they drew were more than enough to ensure that, sooner or later, a new vision of kingdom and church would be earthed in our society.

The other memorable experience was almost the opposite; a feeling that, despite the thrill of what was a kind of "love at first sight", many people were still wary of one another, wanting to test more fully that they were on the same road, and at times were as uncertain about others' destination as they were about their own. This surfaced at the last session of the Congress, when a difference of opinion emerged concerning whether those present ought to support the establishment of the Community Resources Centre as a formally constituted body with charitable status. Though the debate focused on the future organization and role of the Centre, the discussion revealed a deeper concern: should basic Christian groups remain informally and loosely linked together, or was a more corporate and manifest form of movement required, to which they should give overt allegiance and active support?

Despite such differences of opinion, I came away from

the 1980 Community Congress certain that a new vision of
the kingdom was abroad, and that a movement to bear
witness to it was being born, though its growth and development could well be a long and painful process.

From 1980 onwards the Community Resources Centre,
and the National Centre for Christian Communities and
Networks (NACCCAN for short) which succeeded it in
1981, continued to service the growing community
movement. Those of us at the Centre had the privilege of
being in close touch with what was happening throughout
the country. It also enabled us to recognize more easily than
most how the vision of the kingdom community evident at
the 1980 Congress could easily be distorted or compro-
mised. Over the next few years, therefore, we had to
counter a number of challenges which, from our vantage
point at least, would have weakened the community
movement. Most challenges came from those who had
grasped part of the vision but then sought, some more
militantly than others, to insist that it was the whole of the
picture.

The National Centre's first challenge came from groups
which asserted that the zenith of community was living
together under one roof and sharing all things in common.
It was mainly from this section of the Congress that the
resistance to a national resource unit emerged. It was true
that "intentional communities", as with the early secular
communes, had played a major role in bringing the issue of
community to the fore. I had myself learnt an immense
amount from the numerous courageous experiments.[52] But
we did not think that they should be seen as the ultimate
norm. For one thing, relatively few people had the
opportunity to live in this way. For another, the kingdom
community was not just about closer relationships, however
important, but about a spectrum of outgoing ministries,
only some of which required a residential base.

To hold on to what we saw as the fuller picture was not

easy. For example, the title of the "National Centre for Christian Communities and Networks" was not what I myself wanted. I would have preferred to have dispensed with the word "communities" altogether, as I felt that it played into the hands of those (some because they sincerely believed it to be the case, but others because they could then write off the movement as little more than a group of hippies) who took the search for community to be above all else about communal living.

As a compromise, the words "communities" and "networks" were both included. Unfortunately, it has still led to NACCCAN being assumed by many to be a counselling and advice centre for those, sometimes with major personal problems, wanting to live in community. On the other hand, it has had the advantage of helping the religious orders to identify more closely with us.

A related problem emerged in connection with regional gatherings, held since 1980 in the South, the Midlands, South Wales, Scotland and Northern Ireland, which by and large have attracted those interested in communal living. Because of this, such conferences have often been attended by a relatively narrow section of the community movement.

The second challenge to a holistic view of the kingdom community was typified by a NACCCAN conference set up in 1983 to explore those characteristics that basic Christian groups in the United Kingdom and "basic ecclesial communities" in Latin America did or did not hold in common. The protest at this event came from those who dismissed the initiatives on the home scene, and the "basic community" label sometimes given to them, as a betrayal of the poor and marginalized, who alone were assumed to make up the true Christian community movement. In some ways it was a pertinent criticism. In Latin America, the (Roman Catholic) faith was still strongly in evidence amongst the disadvantaged and oppressed, and basic ecclesial communities thus included many from this stratum of the population. In contrast, on the European continent as well as in the United Kingdom the community movement consisted mainly of middle-class Christians. None the less, though fully believing that the community movement must have "an option for the poor", we could see no reason to devalue the endeavours of the less poor in the process.

Many of these had made considerable sacrifices to pursue their vision, many were socially if not materially marginalized, and virtually all sought to stand with the poor. For us, such groups remain an integral part of those in search of the kingdom community, though they need to be especially open to reviewing their lifestyle and actions in the light of the situation of those less privileged.

A third challenge to NACCCAN has come from those, also following the Latin American model, who see basic Christian groups as a heaven-sent means of renewing the life of the parish. Their role is to breathe new life into the dry bones of the local church. As I shall point out in the next chapter, the community movement has a great deal to offer in this respect, not least in enabling the church to regain a foothold in areas of multi-deprivation. Yet its role is more all-embracing and disturbing than simply seeking to put the parish back on its feet.

In contrast, a fourth challenge has come from those who see the pursuit of key issues of the day as the all-important means of furthering the coming of the kingdom. Who can deny this? Are not issues of race, gender, class and, perhaps above all, peace, of fundamental importance for the future of our world? When NACCCAN came into being, we held a number of consultations seeking to enable groups to network around such issues.[53] At the 1980 Congress, and at a second Congress held in 1984, we deliberately set up a number of workshops on matters of social and political concern. At the 1984 Congress these were supplemented by five "centres" open throughout the event, one of which majored on peace and justice, and one on women's rights.

The Management Committee of NACCCAN has also sought to include representatives of issue-centred groups.

The danger here, however, is that those intensely committed to a single issue can find it so all-consuming that they fail to see the panorama, and thus the significance, of the Christian community movement as a whole. They can so stress diversity that they forget interdependence. They can so emphasize the importance of their cause that they have no time to listen to and share with their fellow Christians in search of the same kingdom. They can be so concerned with issues that they neglect community. This gravely weakens not only the movement as a whole, but prevents their drawing on valuable experience and resources to help them in their own task.

A further challenge has come from the tenacity of a denominational and divided church. The Management Committee of NACCCAN is one of the most ecumenical national bodies in the country, with Roman Catholics and Quakers being full members alongside many other denominations. The two national Congresses, and other gatherings, have seen a representation from all churches. Yet the assumption that denominational demands always take priority, and the inability to recognize our interdependence as a kingdom community, are ever present.

This has been noticeable within the religious orders. From the Hengrave Hall conference, and through the 1980 Community Congress, many orders, both Roman Catholic and Anglican, appeared greatly enthused by contact with basic Christian groups and eager to share in their journey. They demonstrated this, amongst other ways, by giving generously to the work of NACCCAN. But, bit by bit, denominational perspectives seem to have re-asserted themselves, perhaps with the disappearance of some more enlightened Provincials, and the old priorities have re-emerged. There are notable and encouraging exceptions, but many orders, their charisma tamed long ago by the institutional church, have been unable to rekindle it, and to play the key role that should be theirs in fostering a new kingdom community movement. Whether this gradual withdrawal can be reversed remains to be seen.

Another challenge has come from those who bring to a definition of the kingdom community narrow theological presuppositions. There are those from the evangelical wing of the church who want to build the kingdom community as a close-knit homogeneous society founded on a few fundamental (and sometimes fundamentalist) principles. The exciting thing here, however, is that the dynamic power of the Trinity seems to be breaking existing moulds and enabling at least some evangelicals to address themselves not only to the proclamation of biblical truth as they see it, but to issues of justice and peace, and even of Christian unity.[54]

On the other hand, there are those, like the Quakers, who often sit loose to any kind of explicit theology. They are so open to political and social concerns that commitment to an overtly Christian company in search of the kingdom community seems an embarrassment or distraction. This is a pity, for in many ways the structure and ethos of the Society of Friends have a great deal in common with the new Christian community movement. Even so, there remains a steadily growing number of Quakers, as at Woodbrooke College, being drawn towards the emerging community movement and the theology which gives it momentum.[55]

A final challenge, which should be mentioned here, has come from the small number of black Christians ready to be involved in basic Christian groups or in gatherings set up by NACCCAN. The black churches have one of their number on NACCCAN's Management Committee, but this has done little to facilitate wider participation. The problem is undoubtedly linked to a history of often unconscious racism, which permeates basic Christian groups as much as the institutional church. But I believe an even more significant issue to be that the black churches still operate within traditional ecclesiastical forms and, like their white counterparts, neither understand nor appreciate what the Christian community movement is saying, as much to them as to any other part of the church. For that, basic Christian groups, and NACCCAN, are as much to blame as anyone else. Nevertheless, the separation of black Christians from the community movement remains a sad fact.

6. A Kingdom Community Movement

These challenges to the nature and purpose of the community movement, as interpreted from the vantage point of NACCCAN, were sometimes hard to counter. For we, too, could fail to discern the Trinity at work and misread the signs of the kingdom. Yet because of our position at the heart of a national network, we felt some responsibility for searching out the next stage of the journey for the community movement as a whole.

In July 1984, we sponsored a second National Congress of basic Christian groups in Birmingham. Some two hundred and fifty people again attended, drawn from about the same number of groups as in 1980, though this time fewer of the religious orders were represented. It was a more relaxed, celebratory and enjoyable gathering than that held four years before. The five "centres", focusing on youth, interfaith issues, the arts, women's issues, as well as justice and peace, were an important addition and complemented a host of other meetings and events.

Despite the verve and enthusiasm evident, however, the Congress ended with no clearer understanding than hitherto of the message for which the community movement should be the vehicle, of the future form the movement might take, or of its task in relation to the institutional church and wider society. The title of the 1984 Congress was "Live Your

Vision". It was one that brought high expectations. Yet I came away feeling that, although the gathering symbolized a vision of great importance, few people had really grasped its substance. There was little indication that the groups represented at the Congress were yet that "prophetic community" about which John Davies had written so perceptively in *Community* magazine a few months before.[56]

In September 1984, with the support of my college, I became Director of NACCCAN on a half-time basis for an intitial period of two years. This was a demanding task and without the support of NACCCAN's very able Administrator, Pat Priestly, it would have been an even more difficult one. It was not simply that the calls on the time and energy of an under-funded and under-staffed resource centre were growing apace. It was that I was myself unsure which direction the community movement was being called to take, and thus what role NACCCAN should be playing in relation to it. I now believe we took a "wrong" turning.

This "wrong" turning was not so much a cul-de-sac as a foray into foreign territory which proved premature. I was sure that, sooner or later, the community movement had to address itself to the challenge of the transformation of secular institutions as well as of the church. But most basic Christian groups still remained on the margins or within the cracks. The nearest that many of them had come to confronting political, economic and social systems with the values of the kingdom community was the pursuit of issues such as peace, human rights and poverty. This was important, but public decision-makers remained virtually untouched and Christians struggling to bear witness to the nature of the kingdom within secular institutions isolated and unsupported. Thus I believed NACCCAN should seek to promote the growth of basic Christian groups and of networks within institutions themselves.

For a year or more I put a good deal of effort into this task. In autumn 1984, *Community* magazine began to feature short articles entitled "View from the Institutions", written by those in the thick of the mainstream life of society – head teachers, doctors, civil servants, probation officers, industrialists, community workers, planning officers and so forth. NACCCAN set up a series of consultations attempting to draw Christians working in the secular sectors together. A few of these were well attended, but by and large the endeavour was a failure. The lack of response to a more broadly based event entitled "Christians hard at work in a cold climate" proved conclusively that the hour had not yet come for this kind of initiative. Neither lay people working within secular institutions, nor the church, nor NACCCAN, nor (more significantly) the community movement, were ready for such an unexpected and apparently radical development.

The failure of this premature attempt to gather and catalyse the kingdom community movement within institutions led to our taking stock of the situation once more. NACCCAN's Management Committee set up a working party to review the Christian community scene on their behalf. Observations were also fed back to us by a Roman Catholic sister from Our Lady of the Missions who, early in 1986, had been allowed by her Provincial to travel the country on behalf of NACCCAN and talk to groups about their hopes for the future. The situation was further clarified by written returns we received from some forty groups in response to a study course entitled "What on earth is the church for?", part of a nationwide ecumenical programme of reflection on that issue held during Lent 1986.[57]

So where next for the Christian community movement? I believe that this movement in the United Kingdom is now approaching a difficult stage of the journey. First, there is the issue of it making little impact as yet on the secular

institutions of our society. Secondly, there is the problem of
it making little impact so far on the institutional church.
Thirdly, the movement's message still lacks clarity and
decisiveness, and the sense of corporate identity and commitment is still relatively weak.

I am convinced that to begin to meet these challenges, the
network has to become a movement in the manifest and
fullest sense of that term. It will otherwise gradually fade
from the scene and, for our generation at least, have proved
an interesting but passing phenomenon. Networking has
been important, but it is no longer enough. The development of an identifiable and purposeful movement is now a
human and, I believe, a divine imperative.

I feel sure that basic Christian groups of all shapes and
sizes, of all denominations, with all kinds of ministries, and
in all parts of the United Kingdom, are now being called to
take another step to help further the coming of the kingdom
community. Our response to that call will depend on
whether, in line with the theme of the 1984 Congress, we
have seen the vision and are prepared to live it.

For me, it is a vision of the kingdom community as of
paramount importance in and for our time. It is a vision of
life, liberation and unity for the world in which we live. It is
also a vision of life, liberation and unity for the church, the
chosen servant and herald of the kingdom community. Such
a vision means that priority has to be given to those denied
life, freedom and justice by the powers of evil that seek to
destroy the kingdom community. It is a vision of a new and
dynamic wholeness, in which distinctiveness and interdependence are honoured, and which exists through an open
and passionate exchange of life.

This vision must find a theology which can give it clarity
and coherence. I see this as being grounded in the symbol of
the Trinity, the divine community, three distinct Persons
yet One, engaging in a continuous exchange of life and
founded on eternal love. But such a theology has to be

forged out of the experience of all those groups involved; no one can in the end speak for them.

The vision has to have a spirituality which brings the divine and the human intimately together, and offers the resources of grace essential for the journey ahead. It has to embrace forms of worship and prayer which reflect the vibrant nature of the kingdom community, and not the failing energy of declining institutions.

The vision has to be earthed in social forms which can preserve the vitality and power of the human scale; cells which, however small, contain the seeds of new life and new growth. It has to find a day-to-day style of life which demonstrates in practice what it proclaims about such matters as stewardship, autonomy and human rights.

Yet even this is not enough. A new birth can only come about where there is a commitment to the giver of the vision, the Three in One which is its source. A new beginning can only be made where there is, also, a commitment to others seeking to build the kingdom community "on earth as in heaven". This could well involve those groups identified with the community movement entering into some form of "covenant" through which they pledge themselves, with the divine community, to discover, proclaim and work out in practice, the meaning of life together. Only then, I believe, will the next stage of the journey get underway.

This stage of the journey will be one which will take us through the wilderness as well as towards "the Promised Land". It will mean travelling with many we do not as yet recognize as companions, as well as with those we already respect and trust. But no one else can make the journey on our behalf. The building of the kingdom community is not the responsibility of some "super" individual, group or organization "out there", it is the responsibility of each and every person. If we fail to heed this call then our society will be robbed of the vision and power which alone can save it from eventual collapse. Without a vision, and those prepared to live it out, the people will perish.

This will mean a new role for NACCCAN. The Centre will need to become accountable to a community movement which henceforth takes responsibility for its own vision and its own journey. Programmes have to become policies. Conferences have to become times for reflection, planning and action. Encounter and exchange have to give way to engagement and change.

A new kingdom community movement has two main tasks. First and foremost its commission is to help transform society into the kingdom of God. But the church is the servant and herald of the kingdom. The community movement's other task, therefore, is to strive to build a church which is able to fulfil that role. The situation is now such that this will mean not just the renewal of the church, nor even its re-formation,[58] but its re-creation.

Early in 1986, I let my hopes run riot and set out in the *Newsletter* of NACCCAN "a dream for the future".[59] It may convey something of the spirit of that re-created church for which I long:

I have a dream that this year we shall put the coming of the kingdom community at the heart of our concerns: a dynamic, pulsating community whose emblem is the Trinity and whose national anthem is the Te Deum.

I have a dream that we shall begin to glimpse that without the presence of the kingdom community all human systems – political, economic, social, educational – are doomed to collapse and fail.

I dream that we shall grasp that the church is first and foremost the servant of the kingdom community and that all else it does is self-indulgence.

I have a dream that this year we shall come to recognize Christ the King more vividly present in the sick, the hungry, the homeless, the unemployed and the persecuted, and see an active response to their needs as a divine imperative of top priority.

I have a dream that this year we shall understand more clearly that in bringing in the kingdom community we are engaged in a continuing journey – costly yet rewarding, dangerous yet exhilarating, with many surprises, yet as fulfilling a road as any of us will ever be privileged to tread.

This year I dream that we shall become aware that new life is bursting out in a million and one unexpected places. That we shall have eyes to see and ears to hear the Spirit's doings, not least through a host of communities of faith – small, vulnerable and seemingly foolish – springing up within our society and across our world.

I have a dream that this year will witness the whole people of God, clergy and laity, taking responsibility together for building up the kingdom community and for the re-creation of the church.

I dream that priests, clergy and ministers will cease the futile and exhausting attempt to rejuvenate the church as we have known it, and that lay-people will cease expecting them to perform such a pointless "miracle".

I dream of a new partnership in which priests and people will work together to bring to birth a church such as we have not yet imagined, to be the true servant of the kingdom community for the rest of this century and beyond.

I dream that this year the whole church will become a place of discovery. That the idea that the few "teach" and the many "learn" dies a rapid death.

I dream of a church constantly open, like the Trinity, to an exchange of life and a sharing of experience.

I dream of a people of the kingdom community with a living, growing, catalysing theology being worked out on the journey towards the fulfilment of that kingdom.

This year I dream that we shall not be bored to death by worship. That the sermon will disappear; that intercessions will become increasingly corporate; that words will give way to music, creative art, drama and dance, as well as to silence; that we shall share more with our fellows than a mere handshake; and that we shall celebrate with joy that the kingdom community is here as well as to come.

I dream that this year we shall become deeply ashamed at the way we spend tens of thousands of pounds on lifeless roofs, gutters, monuments, hymn books, organs and graveyards; and a relative pittance on supporting and educating living women and men, especially those in demanding and vulnerable situations, seeking to witness to the kingdom community in a hostile world.

I have a dream that this year will see the end of our captivity to separated denominations. I hope for no more kind words, tolerant acts, gestures of goodwill. I dream of a real shift of weight from that foot bogged down in the mud of anachronistic traditions – on to that foot still tentatively placed on the solid rock of Christ, the church's one foundation.

I have a dream that this year we shall encounter again the God who is forever turning his world and his church upside down that the kingdom community may come. I have a dream that he may actually invite us to share with him in that revolution. And I dream that we shall be given the grace and courage to accept the invitation.

CHAPTER 5

Re-creating the Church

1. Community Movement and Institutional Church

Basic Christian groups at present exist on the margins of the institutional church. If, therefore, they wish to help re-create the latter, it could be argued that they will sooner or later have to come to terms with "re-entry" into the ecclesiastical system. Writing very much as a sociologist, this was my assessment of the situation in 1984.[1]

That perspective still embraces a good deal of the truth. But I believe it can be misleading. For I would now want to argue, from a theological point of view, that basic Christian groups *are* the church; re-entry is not necessary in order for them to receive that designation. They do not represent all of the church. They do not embrace the whole of the church. But they are still the church. Indeed, I would contend that they bear witness to Dulles' authentic models of church (mystical community, sacrament, herald and servant[2]) more genuinely and more fully than the institution as such.

Basic Christian groups see the search for "mystical community", the community of the kingdom, as of paramount concern. This book bears witness to that fact. They seek to be channels through which are offered the life of God, the liberation of Christ and the unity of the Holy Spirit to all whom they meet, above all the threatened, vulnerable and oppressed. They are thus a means of grace, a living sacrament, for all in search of their own salvation and that of one world. For many basic groups, the eucharist still expresses this aspect of being church, but it focuses and does not imprison it.

Basic Christian groups are heralds of the good news of

life, liberation and unity. They have a prophetic role to play which expresses the nature and form of the kingdom community. This means challenging all structures, sacred and secular, which deny life. This means the re-creation of the church as well as the transformation of society.

Basic Christian groups are also the servants of the kingdom. They are there to "re-present" God as Life-giver, Christ as Liberator and the Holy Spirit as Unifier to our generation. They are no more the whole kingdom than the whole church, but they point towards the kingdom community and place themselves at its service in the dark as well as the light places of our world.

If, therefore, the community movement is church, albeit searching out a new way of fulfilling this responsibility in our day and age, it is not basic Christian groups which should be seeking permission to "re-enter" the institution. It is the latter which should be doing its utmost to affirm and support their pioneering endeavours. Speaking in a Roman Catholic context, Karl Rahner puts the point as lucidly as anyone:

If . . . basic communities gradually become indispensable – since otherwise in the present situation and in that of the immediate future the institutional church will shrivel up into a church without people – the episcopal great church has the task and duty of stimulating and contributing to their formation and their necessary missionary activity. The episcopal great church must not regard them suspiciously as a disturbing element in a bureaucratically functioning organization. If the basic community is really Christain and genuinely alive, the result of a free decision of faith in the midst of a secularized world where Christianity can scarcely be handed on any longer by the power of social tradition, then all ecclesiastical organization is largely at the service of these communities: they are not means to serve the ends of an ecclesiastical bureaucracy defending and wanting to reproduce itself.[3]

Hitherto on the United Kingdom scene, the institutional church has been far from "at the service of these communities". At the top of the pyramid there has been a modest amount of interest in the community movement. One or two members of the Anglican episcopate have given outstanding support, as a result of which in 1985 the House of Bishops recognized NACCCAN and gave the Centre its official backing. At the same time, Cardinal Basil Hume wrote of NACCCAN's work: "I know of no other agency which provides such ecumenical support to the development of small Christian groups. They have provided unique service to the churches since 1981." Other church leaders have spoken equally generously. Yet at the "middle management" level of the institutional church, the community movement features on very few agendas, whilst at the parish level it is virtually unknown. Why is this?

The first reason, already mentioned, is that the community movement itself has not yet recognized its own corporate potential, committed itself as a whole to its vision of the kingdom, and thus attained a recognizable identity. This leaves the institutional church confused as to the message and significance of the movement. Those who have heard about it believe it to be concerned mainly with a rather unusual kind of person who, though not feeling called to a religious order, wants to adopt a communal lifestyle, usually within a residential setting. They also concede that the movement might have something to offer along house group lines, but do not feel this to be of particular importance.

A second reason for the institutional church's neglect of the community movement is that it feels uneasy, if not yet disturbed, by what is happening on its margins. Its investments in land and plant do not lie comfortably alongside a deeper interpretation of Christian stewardship. The centrality of clerical and parochial concerns are challenged by lay autonomy. Denominational boundaries and identity are called into question by a genuine ecumenical movement. As a result, the church warily and tenaciously guards its own territory lest upheaval within should be added to ferment without.

Such a situation means deadlock. It means the denial of an exchange of life, continuing decline for the institutional church as we know it, and a long hard task ahead for the community movement. So where might we go from here?

At the end of the last chapter, I addressed myself to the current situation of the community movement and to possible next steps for it. As the movement clarifies its message, I believe it should do its utmost to remain in a positive and life-enhancing relationship with the institutional church. It should explore every avenue by which communication can be improved and dialogue enriched. In particular it should seek to foster and support signs of the kingdom community now appearing within the institutional church itself.

At the same time, the institutional church ignores at its peril the new church coming to birth round about and within it. It has a God-given responsibility to discern the signs of the kingdom, to observe and reflect on these, to further their growth and to engage in a searching evaluation of its own life and structures in the process.

Unfortunately, two models of the church as institution are still in vogue preventing a realistic understanding of its future institutional role, as well as hindering its adoption of an open and receptive stance to the message of the community movement. The first is the model of Christendom, the other that of the church as ark.

The Christendom model was the first full-scale attempt to translate the kingdom community into political and economic terms. Founded on the Constantinian Settlement, it was an endeavour which lasted well over a thousand years. During this time Emperor and Pope dominated the world scene, at times sharing, at times contending for, supremacy. Christendom only went into decline as a world emerged which – founded first on the nation state and later on rationalism rather than faith – undermined its claim to be the guardian of an undergirding universal philosophy. Yet despite the manifest collapse of Christendom, its spirit lives on. The institutional church continues, even if unconsciously, to base more than a little of its thinking and forward planning on the fantasy that it is still universally accepted and approved.

As Christendom waned, the western church adopted another model for furthering the kingdom community, that of the ark. This consisted of building a sacred society in the midst of a secular society. The church held on to, or sought to establish, its own array of sacred institutions: schools and colleges, welfare organizations, holiday centres, homes for the elderly, housing associations and, more recently, hospices and projects for the unemployed. In theory, such institutions were meant to bear witness to what secular society ought to be like, and to be a catalyst for change by example. Behind this hope, however, lay a utopian belief that the influence of the church could somehow be regained, if not by ecclesiastical domination, at least by a continuing demonstration of the virtues of sacred structures.

The reality is that the model of the church as ark leads us up a cul-de-sac. It takes the church ever further into its own private world, increasingly cut off from the secular institutions of society. By maintaining institutions labelled as sacred, the church absolves secular institutions from responsibility for religious concerns and values. Furthermore, the church is increasingly hard-pressed to finance such institutions. The enforced compromise is an uneasy "partnership" between church and state; but "he who pays the piper then calls the tune".

I am convinced that the only situation in which it is still legitimate for the church to retain major educational, welfare or other institutions and organizations of its own is where a secular society has palpably failed to address itself to obvious human needs. Here it remains important for the church as institution to raise people's awareness to what is lacking, and to act as an example of what should be done. But such endeavours must be matched by a determination to ensure that society takes responsibility for its own members, and itself develops the means of meeting human needs. Thus pioneering ventures by the church should be as short-lived as is possible.

For the church to be able to discern and follow the signs of the kingdom, it must surrender its continuing attachment to the remnants of the Christendom model and to that of a separate and separated sacred world. It has to step courageously into a secular, cosmopolitan and technological society and therein seek out new ways and forms through which it can be the servant and herald of the kingdom community. To this matter I return again in the final chapter.

What this new church will be like we do not know. Some argue that we should not even try to look into the future. To me such a view not only denies the divine gift of reason and reflection, but encourages us to ignore and devalue both the signs of the kingdom community already amongst us, and thus our responsibility to prepare the way for the kingdom to come.

The message of a re-created church will, I believe, be very similar to that of the community movement – life, liberation and unity – with priority given to any who are most obviously denied those gifts of the Trinity. The form of the new church will be that through which this message can most authentically and effectively be expressed.

In what follows I look at the form this church might take. I do so by drawing on the experience of the community movement, but pay particular attention to the signs of the kingdom, present and potential, emerging from within the institutional church itself. Any suggestions I make about the shape of things to come require full and frank debate. The kingdom community is not the brainchild of social scientists or even theologians, though I hope it has room for both. But a few practical markers may assist us in getting our bearings. The re-creation of any institution, not least the church, cannot for ever remain a figment of the imagination, however fertile. All visions worth their place in history have to be earthed, messy and incomplete as the results always are.

2. Groups and Networks

One of the most important things that the community movement has to say about the re-creation of the church is that basic Christian groups and networks will become of increasing importance. None the less, they are not ends in themselves. They are one means through which Christians can bear witness to the power and purpose of the Trinity and help build the kingdom community.

The basic Christian group will be of great significance in the church of the future because, as most major religious renewal movements have shown, it can provide a microcosm of the kingdom community, wherein life, liberation and unity can be found and nurtured. It can offer the inspiration and energy needed to re-build the church as the servant and herald of the kingdom, and give it the strength and resources for the journey ahead. The Christian cell is tenacious and mobile, and thus an ideal base for mission in a secular and often hostile world.

But the church also needs networks if it is to equip itself for ministry and mission in the modern world. Networks are not just to facilitate contact and the flow of information and ideas, though these are important. They exist to prevent small groups turning in on themselves, and to bring them to a greater awareness of their corporate responsibility for the re-creation of the church and the transformation of society.

Basic Christian groups and networks which have in recent times emerged within the institutional church are not easy to find, be they concerned with neighbourhood ministry, topical issues or a Christian presence within secular institutions.

Many congregations spawn a variety of groups and organizations. But few of these have any clear commitment to furthering the kingdom community. In many instances the potential is there, yet the secularization of society has also meant the secularization of many organizations associated with the local church.

At neighbourhood level, the institutional church has so far been most active in promoting basic Christian groups of the support type. The house group, fellowship or "house church" could be said to fall into this category. (The "house church" as used here must not be confused with a recent movement of independent congregations taking the title "house churches".[4]) The pioneer of house churches within the institution is generally regarded as being Ernest Southcott, a Leeds parish priest, who in the 'fifties encouraged the formation of eucharistic groups in the homes of his parishioners. These gathered for discussion and prayer, and regularly celebrated communion.[5] They also met for a meal and socializing.

The most determined push towards establishing "the church in the house" came in the 'sixties, mainly amongst Protestants. Many house churches originated and have continued to arise from Lent study groups. Four or five such groups were associated with my Woodhouse churches. In 1965, the Anglicans' Lent programme entitled "No Small Change" involved some 200,000 participants in group Bible study. Two years later, the British Council of Churches drew some 80,000 people into ecumenical groups for a course of "The People Next Door", which highlighted the needs of the Third World. In the 'seventies a number of churches, notably Anglican or Baptist, which were experiencing charismatic renewal established ongoing house fellowships. Lent or Advent house groups, often ecumenical, have also continued to figure as support groups of a temporary kind. But, generally speaking, the 'seventies and early 'eighties brought only limited growth of the church in the house.

Not until their National Pastoral Congress in 1980 did Roman Catholics begin to advocate publicly and forcefully the development of small groups to facilitate parish renewal. One report of that Congress stated: "We overwhelmingly recommend that parishes should become a communion of Christian communities incorporating small, neighbourhood, area and special interest groups . . . Such small groups, house groups and neighbourhood groups, for prayer, study of scripture, and celebration of the eucharist . . . must be seen as necessary for the building up of the parish community."[6] Yet relatively little has happened since along these lines. It remains to be seen whether the working party set up in 1985 by the Roman Catholic Bishops' Conference, to look at the role of "basic ecclesial communities" on the English scene, will give more impetus to this form of church.

Amongst the most promising, if still modest, initiatives in this context has been the establishment of a number of community houses by denominational bodies. Root Groups, which began in 1978, is an association sponsored by the United Society for the Propagation of the Gospel. The groups themselves consist of three or four people, usually in their twenties, living in community for a year. They share accommodation, meals and finance, and engage in ministry within the parish. Ten such houses are operating at present.

A similar scheme called "Time for God" is organized by the Free Churches. Yet these small beginnings only indicate how much more there is to do.

The general lack of local basic Christian groups means that few networks exist to serve the parishes, other than those temporarily set up to provide resources for Lent study circles. There is a small network supporting Root Groups across the country.

Despite this rather bleak picture, new moves by the mainstream churches to take the role of basic Christian groups more seriously now seem to be gaining some impetus. One of these is the recent inter-church project "Not Strangers But Pilgrims", to which I shall refer again at the end of this chapter. Another move is that to establish a sustainable Christian presence in areas of urban deprivation. Action was pioneered in 1983 by the Methodist Church through its "Mission Alongside the Poor" programme, since when over fifty projects have been established in situations of economic or social need. This initiative was followed, in 1985, by the Report of the Archbishop of Canterbury's Commission on urban priority areas entitled *Faith in the City*,[7] with recommendations that the Anglican church direct more resources towards deprived neighbourhoods. This document includes recommendations that the potential of the basic Christian group, as a means of strengthening the Christian presence in the inner city or on council estates, be actively explored.[8]

Beyond the neighbourhood as such, two important fields of ministry and mission lie open to basic Christian groups and networks: one concerned with key issues of the day, and one relating to secular institutions.

The community movement is a long way ahead of the institutional church in spawning vocational groups and networks engaged in issue-centred ministries. Many of these I have mentioned in the previous chapter, but of them only the Movement for the Ordination of Women and the initiatives taken by the religious orders could be said to relate closely to the institutional church as such.

One issue-centred network which does have strong institutional backing is that linking Roman Catholic Justice and Peace Groups. There is a National Standing Conference of representatives of such groups in each Catholic diocese, which meets quarterly to share experiences and plan new developments. The groups hold a national conference annually. But these and a few other initiatives apart, the church as institution finds it difficult to know how to handle Christians with a vocation to pursue specific issues.

The need for the church to establish an effective presence within secular institutions is even greater than in relation to key issues. Lesslie Newbigin puts the challenge as follows:

> Modern industrial society is a highly complex system of differentiated but overlapping communities in each of which men and women have to live their working lives, interact with others and take daily and hourly decisions on highly complex and difficult issues. The ministerial leadership of the church in such communities must be part of their life, understanding its pressures and its complexities and its ethical ambiguities. Only with such leadership can there develop in each of these communities – be it factory, university, city council, professional association or whatever – living Christian cells which can function as a sign and foretaste of God's reign for those communities. Only in this way can we expect to see visible expressions of the life of the church where the power of evil is recognized, unmasked and challenged, where the sin of the world is borne, where the power of the resurrection is made credible, where a sign of the kingdom is erected.[9]

One would have hoped that the church as institution would be well ahead of the community movement in response to this situation. In fact, both are currently failing badly here.

The community movement, for reasons already given, has not yet gained sufficient momentum to spur laity at work in mainstream institutions to a corporate sense of responsibility for mission. The institutional church has sought to support the ministry of working laity in two ways. One has been through formal Christian associations such as those for teachers, adult educators or doctors. But these have linked up individuals, and then only loosely, rather than led to the formation of vocational groups. The other has been through the service of chaplains, if and where the money has been available. Unfortunately this tends to perpetuate a clerical as well as an ark-like model of the church. Both these approaches to ministry within a secular society are inadequate and increasingly inappropriate for the situation facing the church today. They leave the vast majority of laity isolated, unsupported and under-valued in any attempt they may make to further the kingdom community.

None the less, a few interesting signs of a new approach to Christian witness in secular institutions are beginning to appear. One such, though still in its early stages, is the development of basic groups and a network of Christians, lay and ordained, working in the field of further education. The National Ecumenical Agency in Further Education was set up in the late 'seventies "to contact Christians in colleges of further education in order to encourage and support the development of a Christian presence in the colleges."[10] The Agency now has a full-time secretary and, in 1984, appointed a full-time field officer in the West Midlands. Typical of most networks, it publishes a bulletin and holds occasional national conferences. One of the most important consequences has been the sponsorship by a variety of funding bodies of "correspondents" within colleges of further education, who act as link-persons with the core staff, from time to time meeting together to share concerns. Within the colleges the Christian presence may be identified in various ways. "In some it may be a form of chaplaincy, in others team ministry, elsewhere informal staff gatherings or perhaps joint staff/student meetings."[11]

The importance of such developments in further education is that they are seeking to initiate a process by which Christians of all denominations can be identified and gathered, in order to reflect on and express their faith in a world where secular beliefs and values dominate the scene. It is a model which places the people of God before religious professionals, unity before denominations, and the kingdom community before the church. Although it is even harder to maintain such a network than it is to establish it, and although many more such networks in other institutional contexts are needed, it is an important initiative deserving careful study.

When basic Christian groups and networks conveying the message of the kingdom community do develop widely, the re-creation of an institutional church will be more than a possibility. In the rest of this chapter, therefore, I explore a few changes that could occur within the institution if such a development takes place. Here and there such changes seem to be under way, and to a few examples of these I draw attention.

3. The Local Congregation

Christmas in recent years has seen our family joining my sister's family on the Wirral. My brother-in-law is a Methodist minister. We always look forward to the Christmas Day morning service in his church because it is conducted in such an imaginative way.

The Christmas Day service in 1985 began with Len offering a warm welcome to those present from other parts of the country and from overseas. We all greeted those sitting near to us. Church members read the lessons and received the offering at the communion rail. A family from the congregation lit the last of the candles on the Advent ring. A Christmas poem, written by a church member who had died the previous Christmas, was used as one of the readings. Presents received by the children earlier had been brought by them to church and, on a brief walk-about, Len held them up for the congregation to admire and enjoy. A baby boy, just two weeks old, was presented to the congregation as a reminder that God the Creator was always at work, and as a sign of the gift of his own Son to humankind. Len preached on the theme of God's love made tangible in Christ. At the close, we were asked to express our thanks through a collection for the work of the National Children's Home. We said the grace together.

Our worship that Christmas morning was, for me, a sign of the church bearing witness to the kingdom community: relating, sharing, proclaiming and caring. It was an act of joyful celebration which gathered up and used the experiences and concerns of the whole congregation. It facilitated that all-important exchange of human and divine life, which is frequently denied by the use to which we put our sacred places and rituals.

Unfortunately, we too often ignore the fundamental function of the local congregation. It should reflect the wholeness of the kingdom community, not just one facet of it. Thus worship should be a focus for the adoration of God as Life-giver; it should enable each individual to find liberation in and through Christ; it should be a means of our discovering anew the unity of all things in the Holy Spirit. Worship within the local congregation should lead us to a deep sense of interdependence and of solidarity in and with the Trinity. It should also point us to the continuing needs of those denied life, liberty, and fellowship with others.

This can only happen if we recognize that the local congregation has to be a gathering of dynamic groups and not just of individuals. This is not to say that every single person must belong to a group; but it is to argue that membership of some Christian cell should be the rule. How else can Christians discover for themselves, or hope to show to others, what being members of the kingdom community is all about?

Amongst the multitude of groups which exist on the local church scene – play groups, uniformed organizations, youth clubs, luncheon clubs, women's meetings, leisure based groups, sports organizations – few may be basic Christian groups as I have described them. Yet the possibility of enabling these groups to recognize and own their potential for building the kingdom is always there. This so often remains unrealized because the worshipping congregation meets as a quite separate entity, at a quite separate time and in a quite separate place.

To enable all groups to begin to explore their role as kingdom builders, the local church might take a number of preliminary steps. One would be to ensure that those involved knew not only what was happening in terms of activities and events, but what were the views and concerns of its members. Many church newsletters undertake the former task well; few facilitate a lively exchange of personal experiences and reflections. Another step would be to help members of groups to meet and share more fully. This could be done if more time were taken, probably on a Sunday and before worship, to make this possible. A third step would be to ensure that the experiences and discoveries of each group were regularly taken up into the liturgical life of the congregation and used as an integral part of worship. Here the task of the priest or minister would be to help shape the liturgy in a way that gave it coherence and direction, and did not allow it to become a pot pourri of bits and pieces.

In addition, there should be every endeavour to foster the growth of many more basic Christian groups, probably through regular meetings in homes, to share experiences, to think hard in a biblical and theological context about living the faith today, and to support one another pastorally. These groups might be encouraged to network by sharing news and ideas, perhaps through the help of an itinerant co-ordinator (a matter I shall return to later).

There should also be an attempt to establish a Christian community house in each parish, not least in areas of economic and social deprivation. A resident core group engaged in prayer and service, and a door as open as possible to callers, would be important features. This would offer another valuable model of how the local church can fulfil its communal role within the neighbourhood.

4. The Region and its Assembly

The potential of the local congregation to meet, to share, to celebrate and to engage in mission is far from being fulfilled. Yet even if much more were made of this aspect of church life, another whole area of Christian ministry would remain relatively unsupported; that which at present is exercised in many inconspicuous ways at the level of the town, the city or the region.

This sphere of ministry the church in this country has consistently failed to address with understanding or commitment, at least since industrialization and urbanization. These two great changes set the population of rural Britain on the move. As people gradually settled down again a quite new demographic, economic and political map was drawn. The local neighbourhood had lost, or was soon to lose, much of its communal importance, whilst larger and more cosmopolitan social units became more relevant to the lives of many. If, therefore, the church wishes to demonstrate the significance of the kingdom community for today's world, it is with these new regions, *zones humaines* as they were called in the 'sixties, that it also has to concern itself.

To do this effectively will be a long and difficult task, catching up on many years of neglect. But in the process it could further the re-creation of the church for its missionary task in several ways. In the first place, to raise the eyes of Christians, not least the ordained ministry, from preoccupation with their parish to the needs of the region brings home the missionary imperative. For it is at the regional level that many of the forces which shape human life now operate, and it is here that the principles and practices of a secular society all too often go unchallenged.

In the second place, a church which responds realistically to regional needs is compelled to abandon over-dependence on the parish priest. The latter just does not have the experience, skills and training in this context to cope. The immensely rich and diverse resources of the laity have to be brought into play if the church is to address itself responsibly to the scale, as well as to the complexities and confusions, of regional affairs in the 'eighties.

Thirdly, the wasteful luxury of denominationalism, still so easy to settle for even in the most vigorous local congregation, becomes not only meaningless, but destructive of missionary endeavour at the regional level. Industry, commerce, welfare, health, law and order, and much of education regard the divisions within the Christian church as irrelevant. They have long since learnt to "neutralize" any problems which such divisions might cause them by insisting that dealings with the religious community be of a "non-sectarian" nature.

To further the coming of the kingdom beyond the confines of the parish will require the creation of a plethora of basic Christian groups within secular institutions. It will also mean the creation of networks to enable such groups to share experiences, ideas and resources. It is a task to which the church must give top priority, drawing freely and fully on the experience of the Christian community movement. This task will also require a new kind of regional assembly to replace often moribund synods, and similar regional gatherings.

Most synods at the moment cover far too wide an area (several human zones), representation is from local congregations many of whose members are ill-informed about regional affairs, they are dominated by the religious professionals, and they are conducted as formal business meetings rather than being used as opportunities for lively exchange and debate about Christian faith in today's world. Not least, they are all captive to an anachronistic denomi-nationalism.

A new style regional assembly would be a focus for meeting, deliberating and planning for the building of the kingdom community. It would regard secular issues affecting the region as more important than ecclesiastical ones. It would give priority to the voice of laity, in particular to those involved in basic Christian groups and networks addressing institutional or regional concerns. It would be ecumenical in constitution and membership.

There are as yet no examples of such an alternative model; though it is possible that the Merseyside and Regional Churches Ecumenical Assembly, set up after Christians from six different traditions covenanted together at a "Celebration of Unity" in Liverpool's two cathedrals on Whit Sunday 1985, may point the way.

It is noteworthy that the Assembly's agreed basis of faith is Trinitarian; a fellowship of those who "seek to fulfil together their common calling to the glory of one God, Father, Son and Holy Spirit".[12] Those covenanting together – Anglicans, Baptists, Methodists, Roman Catholics, the Salvation Army and the United Reform Church – are pledged "to God and one another in the pilgrimage and search for the visible unity of Christ's church". This they believe is also "a missionary pilgrimage . . . to unite divided communities and nations in a single new humanity . . . a sign of God's kingdom on earth." In this way the followers of Christ will "begin to express that comm-unity which is his purpose for all."

The medium for this message is an ecumenical Assembly of over two hundred people which meets twice a year. One-third of its number are Anglicans, one-third are Roman

Catholics and one-third are from the Free Churches. The Assembly is also served by a Theological Advisory Group, a Finance Group and a Media Group. It has five Departments – dealing with ecumenical affairs, social responsibility, ministry, education and international affairs – which work through a series of smaller "task groups".

The Assembly looks to be limited in its potential by a number of factors. Despite its commitment to the unity of church and world, the former rather than the latter seems to be the more prominent concern. The fact that many representatives will come from local churches means that, yet again, Christians whose main ministry is to institutions within the region could be by-passed. This neglect is also in evidence in the work of the task group where, apart from the world of education, only three appear to address themselves to mainstream institutions (and even then largely through traditional chaplaincy work). The "equal balance" in the Assembly between laity and clergy, the composition of its Standing Committee, and the existence of a separate Church Leaders' Group appear to give the ordained ministry a dominating role throughout.

None the less, the move on Merseyside is, relative to the rest of the church in the United Kingdom, an imaginative step forward. The churches there have at least set out in the direction of the kingdom community. If the Assembly's commitment to review its structures every five years is taken seriously, it could be a major breakthrough in the re-creation of the church in this country.

Besides the function of deliberation, the regional assembly should also be a place for the celebration of the whole life of the area which it represents. There should be particular occasions on which the ministry of Christians working within the life of the secular institutions of the region is affirmed. At least once a year there should be a regional congress and festival, perhaps lasting a week, when local congregations are called to meet, to share their concerns and to worship together. In this way Christians in a region would be given the chance to identify with one another, encouraged by the visible sign of their corporate presence, and enabled to celebrate together their common calling as servants and heralds of the kingdom community.

The regional assembly should, also, be one to which those of other faiths, or of no faith, receive an open invitation. It should be a place where those who are in their own way in search of the kingdom community, can come to reflect, to talk and, if they so wish, to worship.

There are at present only a few examples of such assembly points within the institutional church, and where they do exist they are denominational. One of the most impressive models is Coventry Cathedral. Destroyed by bombing in 1940, it was rebuilt in modern style and consecrated in 1962. Since then, Coventry Cathedral has focused its ministry on the total life of the city, and on the experiences both have gone through. The Cathedral has also become an international centre of reconciliation and hope, represented by its architectural features and furnishings as well as by the many activities and events which take place there.

The Cathedral offers hospitality to all and sundry, from the Good News Singers of Houston, Texas, to the Girl Guide Association, from the Swedish Waermland Ensemble to the Mother's Union. It is used for annual services by magistrates and bankers, social workers and judges. It is a place where classical concerts and rock musicals, drama and dance, and exhibitions showing the life and work of everyone from invalid children to the elderly, can find a home.

Its worship likewise embraces a rich variety, from meditations to pilgrimages, from vigils to a "Holy Fools Weekend" led by a troop of clowns. And beyond the life of the city itself, the Cathedral reaches out through such associations as the Community of the Cross of Nails, which links over sixty centres of reconciliation of all denominations throughout the world. It is not without interest that its annual magazine describing "Coventry Cathedral in Action" has the title *Network*.

The Cathedral inevitably has its problems. It is so much a symbol of international renown that energy can be drawn away from active engagement in the life of the region itself. It can be a place of passage rather than a genuine meeting point. It can become a massive visual aid to foster the secular education of visitors and students rather than a place for divine encounter. It can become clergy-led, with its laity involved mainly as assistants or onlookers. Even so, Coventry Cathedral has accepted its role as a regional focus of the faith with vivid imagination, enthusiasm and commitment, and it remains a model which a church looking for the coming of the kingdom community should heed.

5. The Laity Centre

One of the most formative experiences of my life was a year, at the beginning of the 'sixties, spent at the William Temple College, Rugby. The William Temple College was set up in 1949 as a lay academy, attempting to engage in the study of the natural and social sciences, as well as of political and economic issues of the day, in the light of Christian faith. That the College failed to survive very long after the departure of its first dynamic Principal, Mollie Batten, in 1966, meant that the hour for this kind of initiative had not yet come – but come it must if the church is to fulfil its calling to bear witness to the kingdom community.

My year at the William Temple College came at the end of my preparation for ordination; it could not have been more stimulating. There were half-a-dozen staff, and some twenty long-term students, coming not only from the United Kingdom, but from West Germany, the United States, Central Africa and Brazil. These were joined throughout the year by another two dozen or more attending short consultations, from industry, the social services, education and the church itself. In all some one thousand students passed through the college in an academic year. Many of these would not have called themselves Christians, but came out of interest or genuine curiosity.

The College's aim was "to relate the Christian interpretation of man's life to the understanding of our contemporary world".[13] This was achieved in a number of ways. There was an excellent library which contained not only a comprehensive theological section, but many volumes on the social sciences and on contemporary issues. The College provided an important rallying point for those wishing to meet others with similar concerns. Such encounters took the form of gatherings related to the work of the professions mentioned above, as well as three weekends given over to an exploration of the Christian faith in relation to fields such as history, physics, technology, human growth and development, and sociology. The college also engaged in a number of research projects concerning how Christian faith could be expressed in thought and action in today's world.

This factual description does scant justice to the key ingredient in the life of the college, the vigorous debates amongst Christians and non-Christians about faith and life. It was a centre of discovery and growth for all who came. Enriching the intellectual cut and thrust were the many warm and open relationships built amongst students, as well as the regular round of daily worship. It was hard work; it was immensely challenging; it was very exciting.

I am certain that the church of the future must have similar centres, though probably on a more modest scale, in every region throughout the country. They must be accessible, open and welcoming meeting places for the laity of each human zone, concerned with the contemporary issues and the life of modern institutions. Furtherance of the work of basic Christian groups and networks, especially those of a vocational kind, should be one of their major concerns. They should be resource centres gathering and disseminating information about the life of each region relevant to Christian witness therein. They should have facilities to encourage informal meetings. They should be places for the setting up of more structured consultations about the affairs of each region. They would offer training facilities for those working on the interface of church and society, a role I explore below. Research would feature on their agendas.

There are numerous "laity centres" throughout the United Kingdom: the Centre for Theology and Public Issues, in Edinburgh; the Arthur Rank Centre, Stoneleigh; St George's House, Windsor; the Scottish Churches House; the Luton Industrial College; the Manchester Christian Institute; the Inter-Face Academy, Essex; Coleg Trefeca in South Wales; Woodbrooke, the Quaker Study Centre in Selly Oak; Ammerdown near Bath; and Upholland Institute, to name but a few. Many are doing an excellent job in their chosen spheres, but all of them fail on one or other criterion to live up to the sort of centre I have in mind.

First and foremost, few are sufficiently regional in their concerns. Many exercise a far-flung ministry, but it weakens their contribution to the regeneration of lay life and witness in the regional context. Because of this, generalized reflection and debate appear high on the agenda, but the support of basic groups and networks in the region itself or help in mounting an active Christian response to specific issues (such as the closing of a factory, a local race riot, sex discrimination by a local authority, ecological neglect in a particular planning scheme, and so forth) is virtually ruled out.

A second problem is that such centres cater more for the ecclesiastical than the lay world. Laity may attend, but it is often their church-centred roles that loom largest on the courses offered. The concerns of the institutional church again predominate; the problems of the layman struggling to be a Christian in an alien and sometimes hostile environment are neglected.

A third weakness is that such laity centres, even where they exercise a more regional ministry, are not sufficiently comprehensive in their work. They have expertise in the field of industrial relations *or* social welfare *or* health *or* education, but are unable to address themselves to the life of the region as a whole. Half a loaf is better than none. But if the vision of the kingdom community is that of human wholeness, of planet, individual and society, then any genuine exchange of life has to cross secular as well as sacred boundaries. This could be done more easily if such centres offered a rallying point for vocational groups and networks active in the region, rather than sought to prove their worth by initiating their own consultations and conferences, or producing their own academic blueprints for the future. This would require centres to take on staff with different skills and different attitudes from those evident at the moment.

Finally, such centres remain limited by their denominational affiliations and commitments. As part of the Established Church, Anglican centres here command more universal support than most. But sooner or later a restrictive denominational approach has to give way to the genuinely ecumenical laity centre if the work of the kingdom community is to be furthered.

Overcoming these problems is the next stage of growth for the laity centre wanting to play a major role in a re-created church. Until this happens personnel, expertise and resources will be wasted, and an all-important regional meeting ground for Christians at work in a secular society will remain undeveloped.

6. Leadership

The re-creation of the church will require the re-creation of its leadership. Of all the challenges facing us as Christians, ordained and lay alike, this is amongst the toughest. Past patterns of leadership are so deeply rooted and firmly established that it is extremely difficult for anyone to conceive of anything very different from what is the norm today. Yet without fundamental changes in this quarter there will be little movement forward elsewhere.

My concern at this point is the role and practice of those called, trained and commissioned to be the paid servants of the church locally, regionally or nationally. I take it for granted that the church as a whole, at whatever level, must move towards a greater degree of lay participation and corporate decision making; and that its new leaders will be totally committed to this.

A new style of leadership is now required not only to reflect the sharing of the authority within the kingdom community, but because the church has to operate as a missionary movement in today's world. Though many clergy exercising their traditional functions – sacramental, pastoral and educational – will still be required, a new missionary leadership is needed to address a different task.

I have elsewhere used the word "facilitator" to describe such a person.[14] Unfortunately this term has in recent years become associated with an easy-going, and even laissez-faire, kind of leader. Thus I shall here use the term "animator" instead. An animator is a person who combines the roles of catalyst and facilitator. An animator seeks to bring about an exchange of life. It is a role which requires experience and expertise, and is a demanding one to undertake.

The overall task of missionary animators is to help form and maintain a missionary movement committed to the building of the kingdom community, the re-creation of the church as its servant and herald, and the transformation of society. In this undertaking I see the animator as having at least nine key tasks to fulfil.

The first of these, and as important as any, is to discern and interpret the signs of the kingdom community in a secular world. This is an undertaking which can only be accomplished by those who have spent a good deal of time listening and learning, at first-hand as well as through study and prayer, to what is going on within the cracks and on the margins, as well as within the mainstream of institutional life. Through such discernment and interpretation animators are here getting their own bearings, in order that they can better guide others in their various ministries.

The second task is to locate where Christians are actually present and active in society. As relatively few ordained ministers know very much about the occupations of their congregations, this information is hard to come by. Even lay people are sometimes surprised to discover, after a long period of acquaintance, the Christian allegiance of colleagues at work.

This process of identification leads to the third task, that of gathering those located into vocational groups. This can neither be forced nor rushed. Because a number of church leaders are beginning to believe that groups might be "a good thing", there is a danger that undue pressure will be put on people to join them. This would be counter-productive. The people of God in the world will gather because they feel it to be a divine imperative, not because they are instructed so to do.

Basic groups will have many different concerns – allowing a rich diversity to emerge is all-important.[15] But if they are themselves to become an integral part of a missionary church the fourth task of animators must be to encourage them to sort out, reflect on and talk through their everyday experiences in the light of biblical study, prayer and theology. The role of the animator is to raise the awareness of those involved to the signs of the kingdom community around them, and to help them to discover what these signs are revealing about their own calling as Christians, individually and as a body.

The fifth task of animators is to offer basic groups access to the resources neeeded for study, reflection and action. This is a pragmatic task and will necessitate animators being in close touch with those able to offer appropriate expertise and resources in secular as well as in sacred fields.

A sixth task may emerge at this or any other point in the life of missionary groups or networks. It is the all-important one of enabling laity to accept both the privilege and the responsibility of being the church in the world. This means those involved assuming authority for undertaking the missionary vocation to which all Christians are called. The animator fades more into the background as the group begins to own its missionary task. However, the change in relationship between group and animator is not so much from dependence to independence, as from dependence to interdependence.

The seventh task of animators is to assist basic groups to plan and take action on either an individual or a corporate basis. Such action has to arise from all that has gone before, or it is unlikely to further the groups' concerns in any effective or sustained way. It is unlikely that animators as such will be involved in such action, but they will need to keep closely in touch with what groups are attempting and how things are working out.

The eighth task of animators is to call the group to account. This is not an inspectoral role, but one of validating the group's endeavours by enabling them to evaluate their missionary efforts critically yet positively. All too often laity are called by the church to engage in missionary type work, only to be then neglected and left isolated. Animators have the responsibility of seeing that this does not happen.

The final task of animators is to "hold the circle" for the

diversity of basic groups they serve. This means ensuring that groups are in touch with one another and able to share news and resources. Creating and maintaining networks is a major aspect of such work. But there is much more to it than that. Animators have a symbolic role to play in representing the unity and wholeness of the church in its missionary task. In this they witness to the fact that the kingdom community does not come through the endeavours of this or that particular group or network, however dedicated or effective, but through human and divine co-operation.

Animators must be mobile. They will be on the move to find and meet up with Christian men and women wherever they are active in the world and wherever basic groups might come into being. It is a lifestyle more akin to that of John Wesley and his itinerant preachers than to the building-based operation of many clergy today. A missionary church requires a mobile task force.

The animator will need expertise and skills appropriate to his or her role. As they will be operating on the boundaries of church and society, animators will need to have knowledge and experience of both the secular and the religious worlds. This will mean a period of training related to secular disciplines as well as to theology. Skills related to effective communication, and the convening and maintenance of groups and networks, will also be important.

One of the key features of the itinerant leadership of a missionary church is that it should operate on a team basis. By nature of its openness and flexibility, the missionary role could otherwise become more entrepreneurial than facilitating. Aggressive, autocratic evangelistic endeavour is the antithesis of what a church in search of the kingdom needs. It is essential, therefore, that those working in this sphere have the support of, and are accountable to, a well trained and equipped team, operating as model as well as catalyst in building a new quality of community life. The further animators move into the heart of the secular world, the stronger needs to be the bond with their own basic Christian group.

That I have given no examples of such a leadership role so far is because few yet exist. None the less, there are a number of those now working as animators from whose ministry a good deal can be learned.

At the parish level, the work of Movement for a Better World encompasses many of the functions of the missionary animator I have mentioned. This association consists of small teams, mainly Roman Catholic priests or members of the reiigious orders, who work in parishes. Over many years they seek to help revitalize the local church by enabling people to build and participate in the life of basic Christian groups, especially of a supportive kind. The approach is one of encouraging local people to examine their own hopes and to explore and develop their own potential together.

At the regional level there are a number of individuals as well as groups taking up this missionary role. One such person is Ivor Smith-Cameron, a missioner in the Southwark Diocese, who for many years has been using his own home as a meeting place for a wide variety of groups – ranging from very articulate Christian men and women to those for whom most religious language is meaningless. The numbers in each group are small, but over the years his ministry has encompassed hundreds of people searching for ways of relating faith to life more purposefully.

One of the most significant developments in this connection has been a growing awareness amongst ordained ministers in secular employment that they have a vital missionary role to play, in promoting the Kingdom community. Rather than looking over their shoulders at the parish ministry and accepting it to be the norm, they are now taking initiatives to operate within their sphere of work as a mission field in its own right.

In 1982, drawing on my experience of the Christian community movement, I convened in Birmingham the first meeting of Methodist sector ministers and deaconesses (those working in secular posts), together with a number of interested lay people. From 1983 onwards this group has gathered twice annually on a residential basis, to share experiences and ideas. By 1986 there were fifty people on its mailing list. It is currently addressing itself to a reappraisal of sector ministry in the light of a major report on ministry presented to the Methodist Conference in June 1986.[16]

In 1984 a much larger, though more loose-knit, network of Anglican "ministers-at-work" met for their first national conference at Nottingham. By 1986 the numbers on their mailing list had risen to well over four hundred, whilst some seventy people attended their second national conference in Manchester that year. Many of those involved are likewise exploring the role of animator with considerable interest.

I am convinced that the new forms of leadership gradually emerging amongst ordained ministers committed to supporting the vocation of lay Christians in the work place is going to be of major significance in furthering the Kingdom community and for the future of the church.

Another important field of potential recruits for the role of missionary animator is that of the religious orders, Catholic and Anglican. Since Vatican Two, many orders have been reappraising their life and work, and a number have opted for a more explicit and itinerant missionary apostolate. The women's orders, in particular, have begun to regroup into small community houses, often located in areas of considerable economic and social deprivation, from where they operate within the neighbourhood on an itinerant basis.

Animators also come from the ranks of those engaged in chaplaincy work. Many chaplains have wide experience of secular society and are already exercising certain of the functions of the animator. But the model of chaplaincy which simply imports to secular institutions the role of "parish" priests, with the dominant emphasis on a liturgical and pastoral ministry, is of little help here. Indeed, it often gets in the way of the task of the missionary animator.

With all these sources from which animators might come, the potential is enormous. If, as yet, only a tentative start has been made towards realizing this potential, there are hopeful signs that a major new "order", with a clear vocation to build the kingdom community within the secular life of contemporary society, is slowly emerging.

One important issue that arises if a new form of missionary leadership is to develop within the church is the basis of its authority. Just as in the past those whom the church commissioned to undertake a parish ministry had to show their aptitude for conducting worship and pastoral work, so those called to be animators in secular institutions and organizations will need to demonstrate their aptitude for that task. It seems, therefore, that another route to the validation of ministry must now be opened up, a route which should be focused explicitly on the vocation of men and women to be missionary animators in the secular world. Candidates might well emerge from amongst, and be recommended for, ordination by lay people working in basic groups and networks within the sectors concerned. Preparation should ensure that appropriate experience and skills were acquired. This would mean a new approach to their theological education and a much greater emphasis being given to "on the job" training. Salaries might come, at least in part, from secular employment.

Continuing support and guidance would have to be offered to missionary leaders so selected and trained. This should be given by the teams to which they would belong. But it should also be offered by those appointed by the church to sustain, co-ordinate and develop this new form of ministry in a secular society. As with the *Mission de France*, this might involve the appointment of a person of episcopal or equivalent status, not only to demonstrate the formal recognition by the church of the work of animators, but to support their endeavours by offering the resources of the church as a whole.

7. The Servant Church

The Christian community movement, which has been slowly emerging on the margins of the institutional church, at present exists mainly as example and inspiration for those in search of the kingdom. Its vision, its priorities, its missionary concerns and its organizational forms now need to be critically but creatively brought to bear on traditional church life.

Certain essential functions of the church as institution will rightly continue: the telling of the Christian story, the nurturing of Christians in the faith, the maintenance of the rites of passage, the training and commissioning of ordained ministers, and the provision of the administrative support necessary to keep the show on the road. But the institution as we have known it, dominated by concerns for maintenance, has to begin to prepare itself to take up a strange and demanding role in a secular world.

This will mean opening itself much more fully to the influence of the community movement, and engagement in an exchange of life with it. It will mean examining its own programmes and structures in the light of the requirements of the kingdom community. It will mean encouraging the growth of basic Christian groups and networks of many different kinds. It will mean exploring new forms of congregational life and regional assembly, and of furthering the development of a new kind of laity centre. It will mean fostering the role of missionary animators and finding effective ways of supporting them in that role.

This cannot be a "bolt on" operation; it cannot even be a "re-formation". For today's church to take mission into its system on the scale and in the way now required, nothing less than its re-creation will suffice. Impetus for this will continue to come from the Christian community movement, the missionary church on the margins. But this must increasingly converge on and link up with similar movements developing within the institution itself.

Indications that this is beginning to happen are already evident. One such has come out of the failure of the institutional church to resolve the problem of disunity. Early in 1985, leaders of over twenty church bodies in Britain met at Lambeth Palace to launch a three-year "inter-church process" of prayer, reflection and deliberation together, on the nature and purpose of the church in the light of its mission. The process is entitled "Not Strangers But Pilgrims". It has so far involved as many as a million Christians across the country, who in 1986 participated in Lent study groups of one kind or another, addressing themselves to the key question of "What on earth is the church for?" Their responses, together with those from councils of churches, local ecumenical projects and county sponsoring bodies, are being collated, and reports prepared. These will be considered at major regional ecumenical conferences in England, Wales and Scotland early in 1987, and at a final national gathering later that year.

Will anything change as a result? This remains to be seen. The most important thing, however, is not the immediate outcome of the 1987 conferences, but the process of "bottom up" reflection and discussion which the programme has initiated. Problems are already evident even here – the input from the planners or from local radio stations has sometimes stifled open discussion, the questionnaire given to participants was simplistic and restrictive, how the collators will select "representative" responses is unclear, representation at the 1987 conferences excludes those engaged in many pioneering initiatives. But these difficulties should not be allowed to negate the fact that, for the first time ever on this scale, the laity of all denominations have been invited to share their views about the nature and purpose of the church in today's world.

This small indicator of re-creation has been given further significance by the opportunity afforded to the community movement to contribute to the same inter-church process.

The latter's organizing team has encouraged the National Centre for Christian Communities and Networks to invite groups and communities associated with it to reflect on the purpose of the church, and their own role in relation to it. These findings have been sent to NACCCAN and will be debated at one of its forthcoming conferences, and at NACCCAN's Third National Congress planned for 1987. The responses will also be offered to the wider church as a contribution to the ongoing debate.[17] The important thing in all this is not just the response to key questions that basic Christian groups will be making. It is the opportunity for study, reflection and above all exchange amongst themselves which has now been offered them. It is a process crucial to the essential task of enabling this network to become a movement.

If the "Not Strangers But Pilgrims" project offers a participatory process that is all-important for the eventual re-creation of the church, do we have any indication of where such a process might lead to at national level? I believe we have witnessed at least one such, albeit denominational, possibility.

On the 6th May 1980 I found myself sitting in the Metropolitan Cathedral of Liverpool participating in the final mass of one of the most memorable religious events of my life – the Roman Catholic Church's National Pastoral Congress.

The mass itself was a pageant of life and colour and music such as is rarely witnessed today. The two thousand delegates from all the dioceses of England and Wales, as well as from official Catholic bodies, and together with many visitors, packed the cathedral. The service was an active "happening", with laity as well as priests involved in every aspect of it. The offertory procession presented not only the bread and wine to the celebrants, and a collection for the Third World, but the recommendations from each of the Congress study sectors.

These recommendations were the result of three days of open and strenuous debate around themes such as "People of God", "Christian Education and Formation", "Christian Witness" and "Justice", which had themselves been discussed in many parishes and dioceses over the preceding year. An hour or two before the final mass, the recommendations from the study sectors had been publicly read out, amidst frequent applause, at a final Congress plenary session in the Liverpool Philharmonic Hall. The "closing declaration"[18] of that session, read by Cardinal Hume, contained many stirring sentences: "Jesus Christ is the Risen Lord. He is for all of us the way to salvation, the truth that never fails and the life that lasts for eternity." "We believe that each human being is of infinite value in the eyes of God; each individual created and redeemed; each individual with an eternal destiny." "We profess our growing conviction of the need for more profound unity with our fellow Christians and we will continue to search for more effective ways of achieving that unity." "We pledge our deep commitment to Christ's legacy of peace. We affirm that commitment to justice lies at the heart of Christian witness; that the first concern of Christians must be for the poor of the world; that all human beings, of every class and colour, whether at work or unemployed, in jobs which demean or which fulfil, are individuals of equal worth to God."

From my own first-hand involvement over the whole event, I can testify that this message powerfully reflected the thinking and resolutions of a vigorous and vociferous laity in all the study sectors of the Congress. Indeed, the sense of life, liberation and solidarity evident amongst so many Catholics, lay and ordained, had to be seen to be believed. For a few brief days many of us present, Catholic and non-Catholic alike, glimpsed the church as the whole people of God expressing many of the qualities of the kingdom community.

The aftermath of the Pastoral Congress was for many disappointing.[19] People power took second place to priestly power, courageous affirmation gave way to words of caution, and old procedures slowly but surely gained the upper hand. None the less, England and Wales' "Second Vatican Council" had happened. The laity of the Catholic Church had declared their mind in no uncertain terms. It was a brief demonstration of what the sharing of authority could achieve. It was a genuine exchange of life. It was a prophetic sign of the kingdom community. The initiative of only one denomination it may have been, but it encompassed a vision of a re-created church which I believe must, in an ecumenical context, become a reality.

The search for the kingdom community that is beginning to prepare the church for its new task cannot in the long term be thwarted. If the institution as we have it does prove implacable, it will be bypassed. As Charles Davis put it some years ago, "The real question . . . is whether the Christian revolution now gathering force will succeed in breaking up and reshaping the present structures or, resisted to the end, sweep past them to leave them as quaint, meaningless relics."[20]

My hope is that this will not happen. I would want to see the community movement, which is gathering momentum both on the margins of and within the institution itself, opening the way for a re-creation of the whole church. But even then the next stage of the journey will have only begun. As the community movement is example and catalyst for the re-creation of the church, so a reborn church must be example and catalyst for the transformation of society into the kingdom of God. This is the supreme undertaking to which all those who take the name Christian are called. In the last chapter I reflect on what such a commission might mean.

CHAPTER 6

The Secular Scene

1. A Tale of Two Schools

"'Religious community' is precisely what Christian faith is *not* about", writes Paul Oestreicher. "It is about the transformation of secular communities into the kingdom of God."[1] He is right. Christian community, the community movement, and a re-created church are all means towards the coming of the kingdom community, never ends in themselves.

To say "Yes" to life in faith and hope and love is to say "Yes" to the journey towards fulfilment and wholeness. It is a personal journey which brings the pain and joy of personal transformation. But it is also a corporate journey – without which the personal journey loses point and purpose – towards "the transformation of secular communities into the kingdom of God". This will mean the continuous re-creation not only of the church, but of every institution and of society itself.

It would take many more books to explore the implications of this transformation for the institutions of British society. But that is not my task. It is an undertaking which belongs first and foremost to those who work within them. I can, however, illustrate something of what might be involved by reference to certain of my experiences in the field of education. For our educational system, along with all other social systems, has to "choose life" and to be transformed in the process if the kingdom community is to come.

This means that the signs of the kingdom have to be

sought out and nurtured within the world of education just as ardently and devotedly as within the church. Schools, colleges and universities, as well as other centres of learning, both formal and informal, have to give expression to each facet of the kingdom community, as well as to that community as a whole, if they are to play their part in the divine purpose for humankind. Education cannot fulfil its role in human affairs unless it works alongside God the Creator of this planet, Christ the Liberator of the individual, and the Holy Spirit as the Unifier of society and world. It cannot achieve its destiny unless it bears witness to the exchange of life, and the sharing of power and resources as of the essence of the kingdom community.

During the years 1970 to 1973 I taught in two schools in south-east London. Though we must always be open to the fact that signs of the kingdom are missed because of our own blindness or deafness, I remain convinced that in one of these schools there were few such signs and in the other many. As these schools have changed considerably since then, and their heads moved on, I feel able to speak openly about them.

One of the schools was Eltham Green Comprehensive School.[2] It was opened in 1957, and during my time it had a mixed student population of approaching two thousand. I joined the staff in 1971, just as the school-leaving age was being raised from fifteen to sixteen. Eltham Green, under a relatively new headmaster, had taken the bold and imaginative step of creating a Social Education Department for its very large group of early school-leavers.

Like every human initiative, this had its critics. But my two years there convinced me that it was a breakthrough in what school as a learning community should be about. I mention here only a few examples of this adventurous attempt at the re-creation of a small part of the education system.

The department was based on the premise, even if not

made explicit, that learning was about life, liberation and unity. It began where the pupils were, even if many were of limited ability, but moved on from there to explore educational opportunities open to them wherever these might exist.

The first task was to make the most use of the physical environment. The department adapted the school building to its own purposes. A number of classrooms were joined together to offer spaces of varying size, and a coffee bar was installed. Desks were only used when really necessary, and mobility of furniture was encouraged. Even more important was the fact that a great deal of time was spent off school premises. There were day-release courses at local colleges. Every week I took groups to visit shops, businesses, factories or welfare organizations. Students worked in local community service projects and local schools. Visits of exploration took place to sites of interest in London. And in a more leisure-oriented context, there were hostelling trips, as well as weeks spent away in North Wales and Scotland.

The pupils had access to a local Methodist church hall, which they were able to use as a workshop for do-it-yourself skills. This formed a point of contact with the local residents who came to coffee mornings there, and were able to see the art and craft work of the students on display.

These opportunities to experience the life of the wider world, on a scale far greater than in most schools, also helped to liberate pupils to fulfil their potential as human beings.

Many encounters with adults other than teachers, were built into the curriculum to further this process. Besides those they met in their visits to places of work, pupils were encouraged to call on and question local residents in their homes. Thus they had the chance to learn directly from parents about being parents, from the widowed about bereavement, from the handicapped about handling handicap, and from the elderly about growing old. They met people of their own social background and those well removed, poorer or richer, from it. Such encounters produced considerable empathy between the pupils and those they visited, helping the former to feel that they were being validated as significant people, as well as having their awareness raised as to what it meant to be an adult in today's world.

The pupils were asked not only to observe and discuss adult roles, but to commit themselves to them. This was done through a programme which enabled pupils to work for a day a week on community service projects – in old people's homes, play groups, mental hospitals, community centres – as well as in primary schools. The primary school placements proved particularly valuable.[3] Well supported by the teachers there, our students found themselves, many for the first time, assuming a challenging yet rewarding position of authority and accountability. For some it led to a genuine transformation of their image of themselves.

The department sought to foster not only the autonomy of pupils but to increase their understanding of unity. I learnt only slowly how insecure and often frightened fourteen- and fifteen-year-olds could be once they were called upon to move out of their immediate circle of peers. As a result, many fourth year pupils did not even know the names of others in the same year. Thus extending their experience of solidarity was very important.

To further this, I ran a series of small group work sessions which helped pupils to deepen and broaden their relationships.[4] We spent forty-five minutes each week in open-ended activities in which the pupils took the lead. The generally creative way the groups handled this freedom made it for some pupils the highspot of the week. Their sense of solidarity was also extended through contact with sixth formers who came in to chat with them, with adults who visited the department or whom the pupils went out to meet, and through their relationship with teachers off as well as on school premises.

The department was built on an exchange of life. Its success lay in the development of creative connections between pupils and their environment, between pupil and pupil, pupils and teachers, and pupils and adults outside the school. The sharing of responsibility was evident in the way students organized the departmental council, ran a school bank, supervised the coffee bar and arranged excursions out of school where they had to fend very much for themselves.

One example of the sense of community created by and experienced within the department was a major production of the play *Zigger Zagger*. This demonstrated the many skills and talents of "less able" pupils, and brought them all together in a performance which turned out to be an exhilarating celebration of life.

There were many problems, many frustrations and many failures, but I left Eltham Green in 1973 feeling that I had been part of a department in which pupils and teachers were striving to say "Yes" to life. It was, for me, a small but important sign of what the kingdom community might look like.

Things were very different during the year I spent teaching before moving to Eltham Green. In 1970 I had been appointed to take religious education at Greenwich Park Secondary Girls' School. The physical environment was as life-denying as one could imagine. The school was a typical Victorian pile, surrounded by a high brick wall, set in the heart of West Greenwich. Inside it was cheerless, though the gloom was caused more by the ethos of the place than by the high windows built so that pupils should not be distracted by the real world outside.

We were literally imprisoned in our classrooms, which were in turn cluttered up by heavy and immovable desks. At Eltham Green the timetable had been turned into three one-and-a-half hour sessions a day to permit excursions out of the school. At Greenwich Park we were restricted to thirty-five minute periods which compelled teaching to be a series of rapid, didactic inputs.

We managed to get out of school twice during my year there, but so unusual was it that most pupils went wild, like young animals let loose from their cage. The only way to bring any first-hand experience of everyday life into the curriculum was through the occasional visitor (the most successful being a blind man, whom the pupils listened to with interest and respect).

Liberating pupils to discover and fulfil their human potential was a virtual impossibility. There was little opportunity for them to experience affirmation other than through their peers or their teachers, although many of the latter became the focus for the projection of their pent-up frustrations. The attempt to impose rigid discipline usually failed, and eating, throwing anything from biros to beer cans around the classroom, wandering aimlessly about or setting fire to paper, were amongst some of the frequent forms of protest. Because of the lack of adult contact, many pupils learnt little about growing up, and remained fractious and ultimately dependent. They were neither given responsibility nor called to account in a mature way.

Nor was there much hope of deepening their understanding of unity. Solidarity remained restrictive. The all-girls nature of the school paved the way for sexuality to be expressed in explicit form – such as throwing Tampax at one another, or trying to shock male teachers by crude graffiti written on the blackboard. Peer groups were small, cliquish and intense. Pupils remained cowed and frightened by wider relationships, and clung to familiar contacts within a familiar routine.

There were few corporate events in the life of the school other than the early morning assembly, which frequently consisted of the teacher in charge haranguing pupils about destructive behaviour. They then departed to their classrooms, determined to work out their resentment on any teacher without the skill to deflect it.

In this situation, therefore, there seemed little opportunity for signs of the kingdom community to blossom and flourish.

The experience for pupils and teachers appeared to be more one of death and dying than life and living.

2. The Church and Education

In this brief description of two small parts of the educational world, I have used the term "kingdom community" only twice. I believe, however, that its signs are being fostered or denied in every such institution. The church's special role is to be that human association called by God to discern, to foster, and to point out all the signs of the kingdom. How, then, can it fulfil this commission in the sphere of education?

One way the church cannot now do this is to try to "recapture" or to "recolonize" the world of education. The days when the church as church could control the schools, colleges and universities of the nation, and perhaps thereby point some of the population in the direction of the kingdom, are over. Also in decline is the credibility of a church which attempts to serve the kingdom by maintaining its own separate educational institutions alongside or, worse still, over against those of the state.

Such anachronisms are perpetuated by a church which has come to assume that it is synonymous with the kingdom, instead of its servant. Thus it continues to put its energies into preserving itself, in this instance in the form of its own schools and colleges, and fails to recognize that the kingdom community is already latent, if not yet manifest, in every kind of educational institution, awaiting those who can identify and nurture it. As a result we have the scenario of a church trying ever more desperately to hold on to what it believes is a "sacred" community special to God, when all the time he is really at work, unsupported by his church, bringing his kingdom to birth in the wider world of the secular.

A church which seeks to remain a society within a society, seeking all the power and status it can muster, is failing to acknowledge that the emergence of secular institutions and a secular state might in fact be "the next stage" in the coming of the kingdom community. It is a stance which refuses to acknowledge the "coming of age" of the educational world as a whole. It is a position which denies that educational system autonomy, and thus weakens its accountability to society and church alike.

The problems created by a separate sacred educational system are increasingly pressing for the traditional church school faced with the changing character of modern Britain. An important question now to be faced is how the kingdom community can be furthered in a multi-ethnic and multi-faith context. What is clear is that the answer is not to be found in one part of Birmingham I know, where two primary schools stand cheek-by-jowl in a multi-racial area, the Roman Catholic school being virtually all white and the maintained school virtually all black. Not only does this perpetuate religious but also racial divisiveness.[5]

The difficulties carry over from church into state schools because the vestiges of the ecclesiastical domination of the educational world remain evident there too. Assembly at Greenwich Park Girls' School was a travesty of the celebration of life called for by those serving the kingdom community; first, because it was imposed by the law of our (now secular) land and, secondly, because staff compelled students to listen to words from a bible and to sing hymns from a book which made faith a farce, or so remote as to be meaningless.

What I saw at Greenwich Park as the adverse effects of religious education on the personal growth of pupils was a consequence of political lobbying by a church which once fought to make that subject mandatory. In such a context, any attempt to communicate the excitement of the search of faith for the kingdom, past and present, was resisted or trivialized, and thus any hope of spiritual development and liberation made impossible. Greenwich Park also illustrated the divisiveness of compulsory religious practices, setting staff who tried to impose them against pupils who were having none of it. As a result, those all-important relationships deriving from an open and vigorous exchange of life, and on which any understanding of the kingdom community has to be founded, were missing.

The church must disengage from the maintenance or creation of organizations or institutions which prevent it being a true servant of the kingdom community. The only legitimate exception, as I have noted, is where the secular world has not or will not provide for the preservation of the planet, meet the needs of individuals who are vulnerable or marginalized, or work for the reconciliation of groups separated from one another by misunderstanding, fear or injustice. Only here, as servants or prophets, is it still right for the church to create its own institutions, educational or otherwise.

But how can a church which surrenders its secular status and power, find an identity, coherence and the resources which will enable it to be the servant and herald of the kingdom community? The answer is through the emergence of small groups and networks which can help nurture, inspire and bring into being a re-created and missionary church. It is through such groups and networks that the people of God will be properly enabled to pursue their many and diverse ministries in the educational world. The task is not that of promoting "church growth", though this may come, but working for the coming of the kingdom community within a secular society, of which the education system is one important part. It is to those who grasp this situation that we have to look to show us the way ahead.

The Social Education Department at Eltham Green was, I believe, given the direction and ethos it had because of the presence of such people. It was not simply that the headmaster of the school, the head of that department and several members of the departmental team were Christian men or women. It was because they shared an understanding, however loosely formulated, of their work as a kingdom ministry; in which saying "Yes" to life was central; in which God the Creator could be found at work in a state school as fully as in any other school; in which pupils, however limited in ability, or however greatly handicapped by their upbringing, were valued and challenged to attain their full potential; in which building mature and open relationships mattered; and in which everyone was expected to share so that the school could become a dynamic community.

The Christian presence at Eltham Green did not take the form of a clandestine cell or secret society. Those holding the faith never met in school hours to talk about their convictions and their values. What Christian support they had came from well beyond the school campus. Yet there were many communications between us, as much non-verbal as verbal, which created a deep sense of common purpose. This was as practical as it was inspirational, with all of us realizing that furthering the kingdom entailed many hard decisions and many mistakes being made in the process. None the less, the bond of a mutually recognized and shared purpose remained a very important factor in the life of the department I have described.

Those at Eltham Green who held a Christian faith were not alone in their wish to build a school characterized by the hallmarks of the kingdom. There were others on a similar journey and converging on the same destination, even if they would not have described these in the words I have used. It is here that those of us who call ourselves Christians encounter the mystery of the kingdom community. Though we have been called to facilitate its coming, we do not own it. Nor do we always make the most significant contribution towards its growth. There are many fellow travellers, carrying different religious labels or none, who help to further that kingdom, and teach us much along the way. Indeed, the fact that the kingdom community is about the interdependence of all things and all people within creation, and the sharing of all our resources in pursuit of fulfilment and wholeness, means that those who call themselves Christians can never go it alone.

What I have found, both within the church and within education, is that those who, explicitly or implicity, have the coming of the kingdom community at heart find a strange but powerful *rapport* which reveals itself in what the Bible describes as the fruits of the Spirit. There is an awareness that whatever labels we bear, we are in search of a revitalized, liberated and unified society and world. Though it can never be fully explained, we know that we are working for similar ends, because the signs of the kingdom mutually inspire us and point us in the same direction.

3. Community Education

The examples I have used to explore the relation of the church to the educational system have referred to a tiny part of the latter. But there is at the present time a growing movement across many schools and education authorities, which seeks to make the search for community its guiding principle.

From 1977 to 1980 I was appointed by Birmingham as a consultant to what was called the Birmingham Experiment in Community Education. This was a six-year programme, begun in 1974, to develop primary schools as a resource to their neighbourhood; and local residents, especially the parents of children, as a resource to the school. The project resulted in the establishment within schools of community rooms for the daytime use of parents and other adults, and a whole range of educational and social activities being mounted which might help to regenerate the life of deprived inner-city areas.

This movement towards the opening up of schools, primary and secondary, began well before the Birmingham experiment of the mid 'seventies. Cambridgeshire pioneered the way in the 'thirties, and Leicestershire, Cumbria, Coventry and Walsall took a lead in the 'sixties and early 'seventies. In more recent years community education has been actively promoted by the Community Education Development Centre, a national resource and training unit in Coventry,[6] and by the national Community Educational Association.

Two things in particular strike me about this move towards a deeper understanding and expression of community within the world of education. The first is how the principles of community education, hammered out by the Community Education Association, reflect what I have suggested are the hallmarks of the kingdom. The kingdom community is about recognizing that God has created a planet whose resources are offered to all, and have to be conserved and shared by all. The Association states: "Learning takes place in many and varied contexts throughout the individual's life", and "Local educational resources, human and material, should be shared."[7] The kingdom community is one in which individuals find significance and grow towards autonomy. The Association states: "The basic aim of the curriculum in any educational setting is to develop knowledge and skills which promote personal autonomy, creativity and social awareness." The kingdom community is about discovering and realizing the unity of the Spirit. The Association states: "Effective community education can only be the outcome of active collaboration between a wide range of agencies in both the statutory and voluntary sectors", and "Education has a central role to play in creating a more just and equitable society."

The other similarity is not so much the message as the medium. The movement towards community education has certainly been given inspiration from the heights of institutional life. But many of its most creative innovations, and its continuing resilience in the face of economic recession and turbulence in the educational world, have come from the base; from individuals and small groups pioneering new initiatives in freeing education from the straitjacket of the traditional school system. At the same time, though with far greater resources, the Community Education Development Centre at Coventry, an independent charity still working from the margins of mainstream education, has been playing a role in its own field akin to that which the National Centre for Christian Communities and Networks has been playing in relation to the churches.

How then can the church relate to this growing community movement with which it should have so much in common? Once again, the church faces problems if it continues to maintain a sacred educational system. This is not to say that church schools should ignore the opportunity to become community schools. Indeed, such a pioneering and prophetic ministry is the one legitimate reason for them to retain their institutional presence within education. But church schools attempting to open themselves to wider community contacts inevitably face an identity crisis. For secular community cannot any longer be defined in denominational terms. A church school cannot, on the one hand, seek a free and open exchange of life with its local neighbourhood and, on the other, lay down conditions which give power or privilege to those of particular religious convictions. It is a dilemma already being found by many church schools wanting to play an active part in the educational and social regeneration of the areas they serve.

As with other aspects of education, the church's response to the community education movement has to be based on the centrality of the kingdom community. At present this must mean encouraging all church schools to go as far as they can in opening themselves to a wider communal vision. It will mean challenging those who fail to do so, as to whether they are hindering the coming of the kingdom. It will also mean building groups and networks of Christians active in all aspects of education, especially the maintained system, in order to equip them to encourage their schools to move towards a more community-related way of working. In 1982 and 1984 the National Centre for Christian Communities and Networks took a modest step in this direction through two consultations for Christians in Community Education.[8] It was a first tentative initiative and a very great deal more needs to be done.

4. The Wider World

The church's understanding of the kingdom community which it must bring to bear on the educational world is just as relevant to other secular institutions. Welfare, health, commerce, industry, law and order, the media – all these urgently need the vision and endeavours of Christians committed to the transformation of society.

There are signs here too of a growing realization that if we deny these institutions their role as communities and as community builders, we shall destroy them and eventually our society as well. Just as community education is coming to the fore within the education system, so there is the emergence of community care, of community health, of a growing concern within industry about its communal responsibilities, of community policing, of community architecture and of community units within television and radio.

It is easy enough to dismiss this emphasis on "community" as the latest fad, or to see the word itself as akin to the contents of an aerosol can which one sprays on anything unpleasant to keep it smelling sweet. But those working within the context of this secular community movement are neither utopian nor naïve. They know only too well that their vision is still indistinct and that it needs to be both clarified and earthed. Yet they are also aware that, unclear as their destination remains, they have in common far more than divides them.

It is vital that Christians, wherever they work, involve themselves with such fellow travellers. It is vital that we share our hope of glory for the planet, for individuals and for humankind. It is imperative that we do not hug our vision of the kingdom community to ourselves, but allow it to be tested in the real world of ordinary people struggling to survive in an often destructive society.

If it is important that a re-created church recognizes and aligns itself with those in every institution within our society in search of the kingdom, it is even more essential that it does so in relation to government itself, be that local or central. Though there are many institutional struggles in which Christians have to be engaged for the sake of the kingdom, it is in relation to the ideologies on which our institutions are founded that the survival of our society rests.

Here it is possible that a deeper understanding of the kingdom community might throw a little light on the major political ideologies of our generation. None of these political philosophies could have survived as long as they have if, in spite of their many weaknesses, they were not given energy by some affinity with the divine purpose.

Thus capitalism at its most creative draws much of its strength from its insistence on excellence, on the rights and responsibilities of individuals to develop and employ their skills to the full, not least in the economic sphere. In this it has been aided by a church which has given prominence to the Protestant ethic. This ethic derives some of its inspiration and impetus from Christ the Liberator, who sets men and women free to discover and use their talents to the full.

Likewise socialism gathers its energy from its commitment to equality, to the right of every man and woman to have their basic material needs adequately met, and to be offered fair opportunities in their search for fulfilment. Thus socialism reflects the witness of those churches, especially Catholicism, Werner Stark would argue, which have stressed the importance of the corporate dimension of the kingdom.[9] Behind that aspect of the kingdom community lies the power of the Holy Spirit as Unifier, which gives such a philosphy much of its energy and momentum.

To these two great political, and religious, ideologies has belatedly been added a third, that of the green movement or ecology parties. Here the insistence is on the preciousness and precariousness of the planet and of its life-giving properties, without which every creature, every person and every ideology perishes. The green movement insists on the right of our planet, and thus of humankind, to generate and celebrate life. In this, Fritjof Capra argues,[10] the green movement has much in common with the feminist movement and women's search for fulfilment as women. As a relatively new idiology, political interest in ecology is clearly not associated with any particular ecclesiastical tradition, though one might argue that the religious orders, in the place they originally gave to the stewardship of land and, during their history, to the role of women, have something of this concern at heart. Expressions of environmental concern likewise have their link with the kingdom community; in this case with the work of God the Creator, the giver of life and vitality to the planet.

I believe that the task of the church is to affirm within every political tradition that which furthers any aspect of the kingdom community. In that sense, it has a place in each of the political arenas mentioned. What it cannot do is to opt for only one facet of the work of the Trinity over against another; for by its very nature the Trinity is a dynamic whole, and the coming of the kingdom community a consequence of the interdependence, not separation, of its parts.

It is where we have insisted on making capitalism, socialism or environmentalism absolutes that tragedy has struck. It is when we have split asunder, in the name of deifying only part of the truth, what the kingdom joins together that the shadow within human institutions has overtaken and destroyed us. Abuse and absolutize right-wing ideologies and we end up with a Third Reich; abuse and absolutize left-wing ideologies and we end up with Stalinism; abuse and absolutize the environmentalist ideology and we might end up with the destruction of human beings in order to save animals or plants.

The church has, therefore, to affirm and give expression to each aspect, as well as to the whole of the kingdom community. In the name of the Trinity, it can no more neglect the importance of planet, persons or groups, than it can forget their interdependence. This is a political as well as a Christian position. It is no weak and woolly compromise, for by eschewing the temptation to absolutize right or left or "centre", the Christian is denied the security of a political home for life. He or she will inevitably be cast adrift on a sea of conflicting political currents, where sometimes one and sometimes another will be carrying society nearer to, or further away from, the kingdom community.

If the overall political quest can be defined at all it is, I am convinced, as the pursuit of a new cultural, as well as economic, vision that will bring into being a world deeply concerned about the stewardship of the planet's resources, and one in which there exists the greatest degree of diversity consistent with a recognition of our common humanity. But any political programme stemming from such a "manifesto" has to be conditional on our discerning and obeying new and unexpected signs of the kingdom. This means that, from time to time, all political parties will accuse the Christian of disloyalty or political "blasphemy", the penalty for which has in the past been explusion into the wilderness and even "crucifixion".

Just as the church must no longer seek to engage with the educational world through a sacred educational system, so it must set its face against any political institution or party of its own. This is not so that it can stand aloof in lofty judgement on those active in the political arena. It is so that it can give that arena proper recognition and autonomy, as well as enable those involved to render proper account to all whom they seek to represent. The church as servant of the kingdom exists not to laud it over, but to help transform, society in partnership with all those in politics, Christian or not, heading in the same direction.

This means that certain forms of political intervention by the church are now inappropriate; for example, pronouncements made by bishops of the Church of England by virtue of their historic place in the House of Lords. This is not to deny the importance or perspicacity of many episcopal comments made in this context. Indeed, in the last year or so many bishops have offered a valuable and at times inspiring critique of those political decisions which seem to be diverging from the principles of the kingdom.

The problem is that the institutionalization of the church's political voice in this way demonstrates its continuing captivity to a clericalism which denies that liberation, and a denominationalism which denies that unity offered by the kingdom community. In short, the medium denies the message. The political voice of the lay Christian, just as much an advocate of the kingdom, is thus devalued; and the political voice of the whole church, as opposed to that of one section of it, is not given effective expression.

The role of Anglican bishops in political affairs opens up the wider issue of the role of an Established Church. It will be many decades, even centuries, before either the Anglican Church or the government of this country will risk the consequences of disestablishment. Yet while Establishment lasts it threatens to make the values of the kingdom community secondary to those of (one part of) the church or to those of the state. As a result compromise, and even collusion, are more in evidence than prophetic comment and action. The growing number of declarations by the General Synod of the Church of England about political issues, is an encouraging development. The boat is being gently rocked. But how far this can go without threatening the rights and responsibilities of Establishment itself remains to be seen.

Other denominations, too, have in many ways now "established" themselves; through state-funded church schools, voluntary organizations, welfare ventures and, of late, unemployment projects. They too run the risk of stifling the political voice of Christians in pursuit of the kingdom. For those who live by the state die by the state (as the abolition of the Greater London Council has brought home to many Christian bodies in that region).

The way forward for the church as a political community must be similar to its way forward as an educational community, or any other form of community. The individual Christian in his or her political proclamation and stance needs to be supported and resourced not by "established" ecclesiastical institutions with favoured status, but by small groups and networks, local, regional and national, which can assemble and disband as necessary, in response to important political issues.

One example of such an initiative from beyond the United Kingdom is "The Kairos Document", entitled *Challenge to the Church – A Theological Comment on the Political Crisis in South Africa.*[11] This is an attempt by concerned Christian theologians in South Africa to reflect on the political situation in their country, and to offer a critique of the current theological models determining the church's activities there. It attacks a "state theology" and a "church theology", whereby government or church seek to usurp the place of the kingdom community, and argues for a "prophetic theology" which reveals authentic ways in which the kingdom might come.

As important, however, is the process by which this document came to be written. Its life began in a small discussion group held in July 1985 in the heart of Soweto. A series of papers was drawn up by members of the group, then criticized at a second and third meeting. A provisional document next "went public". The committee monitoring it "was inundated with comments, suggestions and enthusiastic appreciation from various groups and individuals in the country". In September 1985, the latest draft was published, having been signed by over a hundred and fifty theologians, ordained and lay. It remains open to continuing appraisal and further amendment. Here, both in its message and in the process of its formulation, is an example of the church as a genuine political community at work as the herald of the kingdom.

In the same month that the first meeting of those producing the Kairos Document was held, Wembley Stadium in London witnessed a very different but equally noteworthy event. It was packed by eighty thousand young people for a twenty-four-hour performance of pop and rock music, to raise money to help the starving in Ethiopia. At the same time ninety thousand people gathered for a similar event in Philadelphia, whilst an estimated two billion watched on their television sets around the world, all linked by satellite so that this epic sharing of musical talent could take place. Bob Geldof and his co-sponsors hoped to raise a million pounds from this happening – they eventually raised well over fifty million. "Live Aid", not just financially but in terms of human solidarity, went beyond the wildest hopes of its promoters.

"Live Aid" was not a Christian event; but it was certainly a kingdom event. It was a massive "Yes" to life, and to life together in solidarity with millions of people starving to death in Africa. It stood with God the Creator in his wish to bring into being a planet wherein the desert would blossom as a rose, and people celebrate his gifts with joy. It affirmed the unique value of every individual, woman, man and child, however poor, emaciated or helpless. It broke down geographical, social and political barriers in the name of our common humanity. It emphasized our interdependence as North and South.

Through the power of the media it gave power to rich and poor alike. It drew from millions of people across the world a heartfelt response to suffering and pain, and forged an intimate link between them. For a moment in time, it enabled them to enter into a covenant for the salvation of a world in crisis. It was a happening which, by that very unexpectedness and spontaneity which is one of its hallmarks, gave us a glimpse of the kingdom community on earth.

The church as the servant and herald of the kingdom community exists to discern and to learn from such signs of the kingdom. It exists to glory in such events. It exists to work alongside those fellow travellers who often lead the way. And it exists – but only when the *kairos*, the moment of truth, comes – to point men and women to the God, Father, Son and Holy Spirit, to whom the kingdom community belongs, and who longs, with a passion that we can never hope to comprehend, for his kingdom to come on earth as it is in heaven.

References

Chapter 1

1 Lewis, C.S., *Surprised by Joy*, Collins, 1964
2 See Haughton, R., *The Passionate God*, Darton, Longman and Todd, 1981
3 Wilson, M., *Health is for People*, Darton, Longman and Todd, 1975, p. 117
4 Bach, R., *Jonathan Livingston Seagull*, Pan Books, 1973
5 Lanier, J., *Gestalt Paraphrases*, Malaga, Spain, undated, p. 1
6 Berger, P., *A Rumour of Angels*, Allen Lane, 1970
7 Clark, D., *Community and a Suburban Village*, Ph.D. thesis, Sheffield University, 1969
8 Palmer, P., *A Place Called Community*, Pendle Hill Publications, Pennsylvania, April 1977, p. 15
9 Berger, P., *The Heretical Imperative*, Anchor Books, 1980; Collins 1980
10 Haughton, *op. cit.*, p. 9
11 Tillich, P., *The Courage to Be*, Fontana, 1962, pp. 114–51, 89–113

Chapter 2

1 Hoyland, J.S., *Silent Dawn*, Friends House, London, 1964, p. 35
2 Psalm 148, v. 11–13, *RSV*
3 Seaver, G., *The Faith of Edward Wilson of the Antarctic*, John Murray, 1948, pp. 15–16
4 Hymn 631, *Hymns and Psalms*, Methodist Publishing House, 1983

5 Teilhard de Chardin, *Hymn of the Universe*, Fontana, 1970, p. 19

6 Ephesians, chapter 4, v. 13, *NEB*

7 Hymn 267, *op. cit.*

8 Luke, chapter 7, v. 22, *RSV*

9 Silverman, J., *Independent Enquiry into the Handsworth Disturbances, September 1985*, Birmingham City Council, February 1986, p. 38

10 *Education for All* (the Swann Report), H.M.S.O., 1985

11 Matthew, chapter 25, v. 42–6, *RSV*

12 *To Remind You of the Wesley Guild* (leaflet), Division of Ministries, Methodist Church, London, undated

13 Hymn 423, *The Methodist Hymn Book*, Methodist Conference Office, London, 1933

14 Exodus, chapter 20, v. 3, *RSV*

15 *The Book of Offices*, Methodist Publishing Houses, 1936

16 Schumacher, E.F., *Small is Beautiful*, Abacus, 1974, p. 202

17 Simpson, G., *Conflict and Community*, Simpson, New York, 1937, p. 39

Chapter 3

1 Dulles, A., *Models of the Church*, Gill and Macmillan, 1976

2 *Ibid.*, p. 187

3 Bowden, J., *Voices in the Wilderness*, SCM Press, 1977, p. 30

4 Clark, D., "The Church as Symbolic Place", *Epworth Review*, Vol. 1, no. 2, May 1974, pp. 6–13

5 Foster, R., *Discovering English Churches*, BBC Publications, 1981

6 Robinson, J.A.T., *Honest to God*, SCM Press, 1963

7 Clark, D., "Face to Faith", *The Guardian*, 14th January 1985

8 Clark, D., "Local and Cosmopolitan Aspects of Religious Activity in a Northern Suburb", in Martin D., and Hill, M. (eds.), *A Sociological Yearbook of Religion in Britain*, Vol. 3, SCM Press, 1970, pp. 45–64

9 Clark, D., *The Liberation of the Church*, NACCCAN*, 1984, pp. 37–40

10 *Ibid.*, pp. 40–4

11 Tillich, *op. cit.*, p. 182

* Publications of the National Centre for Christian Communities and Networks (NACCCAN) are obtainable direct from the Centre at Westhill College, Selly Oak, Birmingham B29 6LL (Tel: 021 472 8079)

Chapter 4

1 Leech, K., *Youthquake*, Sheldon Press, 1973

2 Rigby, A., *Alternative Realities: a Study of Communes and Their Members*, Routledge and Kegan Paul, 1974, p. 98

3 *Community*, No.1, NACCCAN, Autumn 1971, p. 1

4 Clark, D., *Basic Communities*, SPCK, 1977

5 Clark, D., *The Liberation of the Church*, *op. cit.*

6 Clark, K., *Civilization*, BBC and John Murray, 1969, p. 7

7 *Community*, No. 41, Spring 1985, p. 6

8 *Community*, No. 33, Summer 1982, pp. 6–8

9 Clark, D., *The Liberation of the Church*, *op. cit.*, p. 103

10 Personal correspondence, 10th April 1986

11 Eggleston, B. (ed.), *Christian Initiatives in Peacemaking*, NACCCAN, October 1983, pp. 55–7

12 *Directory of Christian Groups, Communities and Networks* (Second edition), NACCCAN, May 1984, p. 35

13 *Ibid.*, p. 13

References

14 *Community*, No. 44, Spring 1986, pp. 10–11
15 *Directory, op. cit.*, p. 30
16 *Community*, No. 41, Spring 1985, p. 5
17 *Directory, op. cit.*, p. 29
18 *Community*, No. 36, Summer 1983, pp. 9–10
19 *Directory, op. cit.*, p. 14
20 *Community*, No. 35, Spring 1983, pp. 7–8
21 Clark, D., *Basic Communities, op. cit.*, p. 61
22 *Community*, No. 44, Spring 1986, pp. 5–8
23 Clark, D., *Basic Communities, op. cit.*, p. 255
24 *Ibid.*, p. 21
25 *Newsletter*, No. 7, NACCCAN, January 1984
26 *Report: 1980 Community Congress*, NACCCAN, 1981, p. 10
27 *Ibid.*, p. 30
28 *Ibid.*, p. 23
29 *Ibid.*, p. 35
30 Clark, D., *Basic Communities, op. cit.*, p. 49
31 *Community*, No. 34, Autumn 1982, p. 5
32 Musgrave, R. (ed.), *Theology in the Making*, NACCCAN, July 1982, p. 30
33 *Community*, No. 40, Autumn 1984, p. 3
34 *Community*, No. 43, Autumn 1985, p. 13
35 *Directory, op. cit.*, p. 22
36 Clark, D., *Basic Communities, op. cit.*, pp. 199–200
37 For further details see *Directory, op. cit.*
38 Cummings, E.E., *Selected Poems 1923–1958*, Faber and Faber, 1969, p. 76
39 Clark, D., *Basic Communities, op. cit.*, p. 265
40 *Ibid.*, p. 266
41 Clark, D., *The Liberation of the Church, op. cit.*, pp. 188–91
42 Clark, D., *Basic Communities, op. cit.*, pp. 216–64
43 Ferguson, M., *The Aquarian Conspiracy*, Paladin, Granada, 1982
44 Foy, N., *The Yin and Yang of Organizations*, Grant McIntyre, 1980

45 Clark, D., *Basic Communities, op. cit.*, pp. 303–29
46 *Directory of Christian Communities and Groups*, NACCCAN, 1980 and Directory (Second edition), *op. cit.*, 1984
47 *Community*, No. 12, Summer 1975, pp. 6–8
48 *Community*, No. 18, Summer 1977, pp. 1–4
49 *Community*, No. 15, Summer 1976, pp. 1–3
50 *Report: 1980 Community Congress, op. cit.*
51 *Ibid.*, pp. 89–94
52 Clark, D., *Basic Communities, op. cit.*, pp. 21–57
53 See the *New Christian Initiatives Series*, Nos. 1–6, NACCCAN, 1982–1983
54 Clark, D., *The Liberation of the Church, op. cit.*, pp. 170–4
55 *Ibid.*, pp. 167–70
56 *Community*, No. 37, Autumn 1983, pp. 1–3
57 These have now been collated into a booklet entitled *Towards a New Vision of Church* and published by NACCCAN, September 1986
58 Full title of Clark, D., Liberation of Church, *op. cit.*, i.e. *The Liberation of the Church – The role of basic Christian groups in a new re-formation*
59 *Newsletter*, No. 13, NACCCAN, January 1986

Chapter 5

1 Clark, D., *The Liberation of the Church, op. cit.*, pp. 153–5
2 Dulles, *op. cit.*
3 Rahner, K., *The Shape of the Church to Come*, SPCK, 1974, pp. 114–15
4 Clark, D., *The Liberation of the Church, op. cit.*, pp. 87–91
5 Southcott, E., *The Parish Comes Alive*, Mowbrays, 1957
6 *National Pastoral Congress Contact*, No. 6, 6th May 1980, p. 3
7 *Faith in the City: The Report of the Archbishop of Canterbury's Commission on Urban Priority Areas*, Church House, 1985
8 For example, *Ibid.*, p. 93

9 Newbigin, L., *Your Kingdom Come*, John Paul The Preacher's Press, 1980, pp. 40–1

10 *Community*, No. 42, Summer 1985, p. 10

11 *Ibid.* See also an important paper by Sherrington, E., *Christian Ministry and Further Education*, 1985, obtainable from her at the Methodist Division of Ministries, 1 Central Buildings, Westminster, London SW1H 9NH

12 *The Merseyside and Region Churches' Ecumenical Assembly*, leaflet, Liverpool 1985

13 *The William Temple College*, leaflet, undated

14 Clark, D., *The Liberation of the Church, op. cit.*, p. 164

15 See *Community*, No. 41, Spring 1985, pp. 1–2

16 See Clark, D., *An Examination of Sector Ordained Ministry*, 1986, obtainable from him at Westhill College, Birmingham B29 6LL.

17 *Towards a New Vision of Church, op. cit.*

18 Congress Contact, *op. cit.*, pp. 1–2

19 Clark, D., *The Liberation of the Church, op. cit.*, pp. 67– 71

20 Davis, C., *A Question of Conscience*, Hodder and Stoughton, 1967, p. 190

Chapter 6

1 *Community*, No. 5, Spring 1973, p. 2

2 See Dawson, P., *Making a Comprehensive Work*, Basil Blackwell, 1981

3 Clark, D., "Social Education: An Experiment with Early School Leavers", *Journal of Moral Education*, Vol. 2, No. 3, June 1973, pp. 243–53

4 Clark, D., "Group Work with Early School Leavers", *Journal of Curriculum Studies*, Vol. 7, No. 1, May 1973, pp. 42–54

5 Clark, D., "Can the Church in Education Save its Soul?" *Bulletin: Association of Religious in Education*, Vol. 2, No. 4, 1985, pp. 64–8

6 The Community Education Development Centre is situated at Stoke School, Briton Road, Coventry CV2 4LF (Tel: 0203 440814). The Centre publishes a monthly newspaper called *Network*.

7 *Network*, Vol. 6, No. 4, April 1986, CEDC (Coventry), p. 1

8 Ross, L., (ed.) *Christian Initiatives in Community Education*, NACCCAN, July 1983

9 Stark, W., *The Sociology of Religion, Vol. V, Types of Religious Culture*, Routledge and Kegan Paul, 1972

10 Capra, F., *The Turning Point*, Fontana, 1984, pp. 23–4

11 *Challenge to the Church: The Kairos Document*, British Council of Churches, September 1985